Workshop on Grammar Engineering Across Frameworks 2015

(GEAF 2015)

Co-located with ACL-IJCNLP 2015

Beijing, China
30 July 2015

ISBN: 978-1-5108-0947-5

Printed from e-media with permission by:

Curran Associates, Inc.
57 Morehouse Lane
Red Hook, NY 12571

Some format issues inherent in the e-media version may also appear in this print version.

Copyright© (2015) by the Association for Computational Linguistics
All rights reserved.

Printed by Curran Associates, Inc. (2015)

For permission requests, please contact the Association for Computational Linguistics
at the address below.

Association for Computational Linguistics
209 N. Eighth Street
Stroudsburg, Pennsylvania 18360

Phone: 1-570-476-8006
Fax: 1-570-476-0860

acl@aclweb.org

Additional copies of this publication are available from:

Curran Associates, Inc.
57 Morehouse Lane
Red Hook, NY 12571 USA
Phone: 845-758-0400
Fax: 845-758-2634
Email: curran@proceedings.com
Web: www.proceedings.com

ACL-IJCNLP 2015

The 53rd Annual Meeting of the Association for Computational Linguistics and the 7th International Joint Conference on Natural Language Processing

ACL-IJCNLP 2015

July 26-31

The 53rd Annual Meeting of the Association for Computational Linguistics and
The 7th International Joint Conference on Natural Language Processing of
the Asian Federation of Natural Language Processing

Proceedings of the Grammar Engineering Across Frameworks (GEAF) Workshop

July 30, 2015
Beijing, China

Production and Manufacturing by
Taberg Media Group AB
Box 94, 562 02 Taberg
Sweden

Introduction

Grammar Engineering Across Frameworks (GEAF) 2015 took place on 30 July 2015 in Beijing. This workshop builds on several previous workshop on the same topic, namely GEAF 2007 at the LSA Linguistic Institute at Stanford, GEAF 2008 at COLING in Manchester, GEAF 2009 at ACL/IJCNLP in Singapore and HMGE 2013 at ESSLLI 2013 in Düsseldorf.

Grammar engineering, the practice of developing linguistically motivated grammars in software, is an active area of research in computational linguistics and comprises contemporary works across many different theoretical frameworks. The fruits of grammar engineering, namely linguistically motivated grammars which in many cases provide rich, detailed semantic representations, support the development of natural language technologies, including both natural language understanding and generation, that derive much more information from the linguistic signal than is otherwise possible. The goal of this workshop is to bring together researchers working in grammar engineering and to advance the state of the art in this field.

In addition to the nine papers included in these proceedings, the workshop featured a panel discussion on how grammar engineering can continue to be relevant in computational linguistics. The panel addressed questions such as, What are the strengths of grammars that cannot be ignored? What success stories do we have? What should be done differently? And what can we learn from other approaches?

We are grateful to the program committee for their thoughtful comments on the submitted papers and to the authors and panelists for valuable contributions to the study of grammar engineering.

Emily M. Bender, Lori Levin, Stefan Müller, Yannick Parmentier, and Aarne Ranta

Organizers:

Emily M. Bender (U Washington) (Chair)
Lori Levin (Carnegie Mellon University)
Stefan Müller (FU Berlin)
Yannick Parmentier (U Orléans)
Aarne Ranta (U Göteborg)

Program Committee:

Krasimir Angelov (U Göteborg)
Pushpak Bhattacharyya (IIT Bombay)
Philippe Blache (CNRS)
Miriam Butt (U Konstanz)
Robin Cooper (U Göteborg)
Berthold Crysmann (CNRS)
Eric De La Clergerie (Paris 7)
Ramona Enache (U Göteborg)
Dan Flickinger (Stanford)
Antske Fokkens (VU Amsterdam)
Claire Gardent (CNRS)
Sylvain Kahane (U Paris Ouest)
Tracy King (eBay)
Anna Kupść (U Bordeaux)
Hans Leiss (LMU Munich)
Timm Lichte (U Düsseldorf)
Detmar Meurers (U Tübingen)
Richard Moot (CNRS)
Glyn Morrill (UPC Barcelona)
Guy Perrier (U Lorraine)
Adam Przepiórkowski (PAS)
Frank Richter (U Frankfurt)
Sanghoun Song (NTU)
Francis Tyers (U Tromsø)
Christina Unger (U Bielefeld)
Gertjan van Noord (U Groeningen)

Table of Contents

Workshop Program

Thursday, July 30, 2015

9:15–9:30 ***Opening session***

9:30–10:30 **Session 1**

09:30–10:00 *Grammar Engineering for a Customer: a Case Study with Five Languages*
Aarne Ranta, Christina Unger and Daniel Vidal Hussey

10:00–10:30 *Building an HPSG-based Indonesian Resource Grammar (INDRA)*
David Moeljadi, Francis Bond and Sanghoun Song

10:30–11:00 ***Coffee break***

11:00–12:30 **Session 2**

11:00–11:30 *An HPSG-based Shared-Grammar for the Chinese Languages: ZHONG [|]*
Zhenzhen Fan, Sanghoun Song and Francis Bond

11:30–12:00 *Parsing Chinese with a Generalized Categorial Grammar*
Manjuan Duan and William Schuler

12:00–12:30 *Orthography Engineering in Grammatical Framework*
Krasimir Angelov

12:30–14:00 ***Lunch break***

Thursday, July 30, 2015 (continued)

14:00–15:30 Session 3

14:00–14:30 *A Cloud-Based Editor for Multilingual Grammars*
Thomas Hallgren, Ramona Enache and Aarne Ranta

14:30–15:00 *Formalising the Swedish Constructicon in Grammatical Framework*
Normunds Gruzitis, Dana Dannells, Benjamin Lyngfelt and Aarne Ranta

15:00–15:30 *Representing Honorifics via Individual Constraints*
Sanghoun Song

15:30–16:00 ***Coffee break***

16:00–18:00 Session 4

16:00–16:30 *Resumption and Extraction in an Implemented HPSG of Hausa*
Berthold Crysmann

16:45–18:00 ***Panel discussion: the future of grammar engineering***

Grammar Engineering for a Customer: a Case Study with Five Languages

Aarne Ranta
University of Gothenburg
and Digital Grammars AB
aarne@chalmers.se

Christina Unger
Bielefeld University
cunger@cit-ec.uni-bielefeld.de

Daniel Vidal Hussey
University of Gothenburg
daniel.vidal.hussey@gmail.com

Abstract

This paper describes a grammar-based translation system built by a company for a paying customer. The system uses a multilingual grammar for English, Finnish, German, Spanish, and Swedish written in GF (Grammatical Framework). The grammar covers a corpus of technical texts in Swedish, describing properties of places and objects related to accessibility by disabled people. This task is more complex than most previous GF tasks, which have addressed controlled languages. The main goals of the paper are: (1) to find a grammar architecture and workflow for domain-specific grammars on real data (2) to estimate the quality reachable with a reasonable engineering effort (3) to assess the cost of grammar-based translation and its commercial viability.

1 Introduction

While statistical methods dominate in assimilation (browsing quality) translation, grammars have been argued to have a niche in dissemination (publication quality). The rationale is that such tasks are often domain-specific and need high precision rather than wide coverage. A recent effort in this direction was the European MOLTO project (Hallgren et al., 2012), which developed tools for such tasks building on the grammar formalism GF (Grammatical Framework, (Ranta, 2011)).

MOLTO also built showcases for a few domains (mathematics (Saludes and Xambó, 2011), paintings (Damova et al., 2014), business models (Davis et al., 2012), and touristic phrases (Ranta et al., 2012)). But these showcases were all dealing with CNL (controlled natural language), which was defined by the grammar writers and designed to be processable by formal grammars. The present paper takes a step beyond these research prototypes, as the language to be translated is not controlled, but naturally written by different authors at different times. The system was ordered by a paying customer to solve a real problem. Also the size of the language is larger than in the mentioned MOLTO applications.

The task was to create a translation system for a web service documenting the accessibility to different sites, e.g. whether they can be visited by wheelchair users[1]. The service provider had a set of text templates written in Swedish, for instance stating that *the width of the door is [X]*. These templates had previously been translated by professional translators to English and partly to other languages. Also Google translate had been used for some languages.

For quality reasons, Google translate was deemed unsatisfactory by the customer. Manual translation was problematic because of its high cost and low speed: the system is updated by new texts continuously, and their translations should appear without delays. Therefore the customer contracted a company[2] to build an automatic system that could deliver high-quality translations faster than before.

This paper addresses a part of the task: a grammar used for translating from Swedish to English, Finnish, German, and Spanish. The translation system parses Swedish sentences (i.e. templates) and generates translations in other languages, by using the interlingual grammar architecture of GF. The translations are manually revised and post-edited, partly because the customer wants to be sure about their quality, partly because the input is noisy and contains typos, grammar errors, and other problems not amenable to purely grammar-based automatic translation. A fully automatic system would require more control on the input

[1] Tillgänglighetsdatabasen, www.t-d.se.

[2] Digital Grammars AB, www.digitalgrammars.com.

Proceedings of the Grammar Engineering Across Frameworks (GEAF) Workshop, 53rd Annual Meeting of the ACL and 7th IJCNLP, pages 1–8,
Beijing, China, July 26-31, 2015. ©2015 Association for Computational Linguistics

language. This was left to future work.

The approach we chose was the "Embedded CNL" (Ranta, 2014): a Controlled Natural Language embedded in a general purpose syntactic grammar. The parser gives priority to CNL analyses whenever possible, but also provides coarser analyses as back-up. This makes the automatic translation robust. Since the system knows which grammar rules are used for each part of the translation, it can show confidence information to the user and the post-editor.

The main questions of this paper are:

- How to best build an embedded CNL system for a task like this?
- How good is the quality, in terms of the usual MT scores and post-editing required?
- Is this approach commercially viable, i.e. competitive with human of translation?

The paper has the following structure: Section 2 describes the text corpus to be translated. Section 3 is a very brief introduction to GF. Section 4 outlines the structure of the grammar and the grammar writing process. Section 5 outlines the translation and post-editing workflow. Section 6 gives evaluation on two dimensions: the time taken by grammar writing and post-editing, and the usual scores (BLEU) for translation quality. Section 7 discusses related work. Section 8 concludes, trying to answer the three questions and give recommendations for later work.

2 The corpus

The starting point was a set of texts in Swedish. Most of them had manual translations in English, many also in Finnish and German. The customer was happy with the English translations but wanted to replace the Finnish and German ones, as well as to create Spanish translations. The number of texts was around 1,900, mostly short sentences of under 10 words. But as the texts also had heavy HTML markup, which had to be rendered correctly in translation, the corpus with tags and repetitions of texts had 26,000 tokens.

The most interesting part of the markup was the **variable**, a segment into which some actual value is inserted when the text is used to describe some object. As the first step of translation, we erased all markup but the variable. As the last step, we inserted it back by using an alignment between the source and the translation.

Figure 1 shows a sample from the corpus. The variables are in brackets. The brackets contain identifiers marking what kind of value is to be inserted in them; the final grammar distinguishes between 13 different variables, which typically belong to different syntactic categories.

After the removal of markup, the number of unique texts was 1,185, word count 7,309. There were 1,258 unique words and 980 unique lemmas, as measured by the morphological analyser of SALDO (Borin et al., 2013). 906 of these were content words (nouns, adjectives, verbs), most of which had precise technical meanings.

In the grammar writing process, it turned out that many word combinations must be treated as multiword constructions, since their translations are not compositional. For instance, Swedish *motsvarande* is literally *corresponding*, but the proper translation of *NP eller motsvarande* is *NP or similar* in English, *NP o elemento parecido* in Spanish.

72 such constructions were included in the final lexicon. This number is relatively low because Swedish forms compounds without spaces, and these were easy to identify as tokens at the outset. For comparison, the final English lexicon has 274 multiwords. Starting with English would thus involve more work in identifying the multiwords.

3 GF and resource grammars

GF started at Xerox (XRCE) to support multilingual generation in controlled-language scenarios (Dymetman et al., 2000). A GF grammar consists of an **abstract syntax**, which captures the semantics of the application domain, and a set of **concrete syntaxes**, which map abstract syntax trees into strings of different languages. As an example from the domain of this paper, one could have an **abstract syntax function**

```
fun Length :
  Object -> Measure -> Fact
```

to model sentences such as *the length of the changing table is 120 cm*. The concrete syntax is given by a **linearization rule**,

```
lin Length o m =
  "the length of" ++ o ++ "is" ++ m
```

This rule is nothing but a string template, which together with the abstract syntax rule is a decomposition of the context-free grammar rule

```
Fact ::=
 "the length of" Object "is" Measure
```

```
avåkningsskyddet är placerat på [object]
the protective guards are placed on [object]

begränsad gångyta är [units] bred
the limited pedestrian area is [units] wide

karusell [exist] som är anpassad för rullstol
roundabout adapted for wheelchair is [exist]

språk vid visning eller guidning [is] speciellt anpassat för att vara enkelt och lättförståeligt
language when showing or guiding [is] especially adapted to be simple and easy to understand
```

Figure 1: Parallel English-Swedish sentences from the corpus.

to a "tectogrammarical" and "phenogrammatical" rule (Curry, 1961). The strength of GF is that different languages can have not only different linearizations but also different *types* of linearizations. Thus for instance `Object` in English is a string, but in German case-dependent string, which is rendered in the genitive in this construction. The German linearization rule is thus

```
"die Länge" ++ gen o ++ "ist" ++ m
```

which generates *die Länge des Wickeltisches ist 120 cm* for the object whose nominative form is *der Wickeltisch*. The Finnish and Spanish rules are

```
gen o ++ "pituus on" ++ m
"la longitud"++ gen o ++"es de"++ m
```

respectively, where Finnish has a different word order and Spanish adds the preposition *de*.

The first GF grammars were small, typically involving up to 200 abstract syntax rules; their context-free expansions could of course be thousands of rules, due to parametric variations such as case. But it soon turned out that writing such grammars from scratch for each application was untenable, as each application had to re-implement morphology and syntax. To relieve this task, the **GF Resource Grammar Library** (RGL) (Ranta, 2009) was created, inspired by the resource grammars of CLE (Core Language Engine) (Rayner et al., 2000). The current RGL includes 30 languages, implementing the inflectional morphology and a comprehensive part of the syntax of each language. The RGL has a common API (Application Programmer's Interface) based on an abstract syntax. Thus for instance

```
possCN : CN -> NP -> CN
```

is a function that forms the possessive "CN of NP" for any CN (common noun) and NP (noun phrase) in any of the 30 languages. The linearization rules of `Length` can now be written

```
mkCl (mkNP the_Det
  (possCN (mkCN length_N)) o) m
```

uniformly in these four languages, by just varying the definition of the constant `length_N`, which in turn can be written

```
mkN "length"
mkN "Länge"
mkN "pituus"
mkN "longitud"
```

using the **smart paradigms** (Détrez and Ranta, 2012) of each language, which infer the morphological properties of words from one or more forms. In Spanish, the argument `m` must be made into a prepositional phrase (`prepNP de_Prep m`).

The RGL has increased the productivity of CNL implementations in GF, so that a system with a few hundred abstract syntax rules can be created in a few days and portable to any new language in a few hours (Ranta et al., 2012). The RGL has recently also scaled up to open-domain translation, due to improved parsing algorithms and statistical disambiguation (Angelov and Ljunglöf, 2014), chunk-based back-up of syntactic parsing (Ranta, 2014), and the ease of building large lexica with smart paradigms. As a demonstration, a **wide-coverage translator** (WCT) has been released as a mobile app (Angelov et al., 2014).

4 The grammar writing process

The grammar writing task was given the following constraints, for reasons of commercial viability:

1. The abstract syntax and Swedish should be built in 2 person weeks.
2. Each of the other languages should be built in 1 person week, including the postprocessing of the translations.
3. Later translations of similar text should be five times as fast as human translation.

4. Each language could be implemented by a different programmer, who does not need to know the other grammars.
5. The grammarians need basic GF skills and native knowledge of the target language, but no Swedish.

Constraints 1 and 2 meant that we had to stop the grammar development at some point and proceed to post-editing, even if the grammar was not yet perfect. Thus the workflow for each target language (after the abstract syntax and Swedish) was defined as follows:

- Days 1,2: Initial grammar, complete for the abstract syntax.
- Days 3,4: Translation + post-editing + grammar improvement loop.
- Day 5: Post-editing to deliver the final translations.

Constraint 3 means that the grammar must be good enough to support faster translation in later tasks. Constraint 4 means that the work can be done in parallel, constraint 5 that the grammar can easily be extended with new languages. In the actual task reported here, the three programmers were native speakers of Finnish, German, and Spanish, two of them GF experts and the third one a student with a basic course of GF covering most of the textbook (Ranta, 2011).

The source texts were in Swedish, but requiring knowledge of Swedish would make it too hard to find grammarians for new languages. Two of the grammarians actually had to work on the basis of the English translations. It turned out useful to write an English concrete syntax to help their work, so that they knew exactly what was intended with each abstract rule. The English grammar was not a part of the deal, but it was needed for this purpose as well as for future use. It was also a sanity check of the abstract syntax: building a grammar with only one language in mind could result in an abstract syntax that is not abstract enough, as pointed out in the "best practices" of the MOLTO project (Hallgren et al., 2012).

The process thus started with the abstract syntax together with concrete syntaxes for Swedish and English. We had two main options for the grammar writing process:

- **bottom-up**: build a dedicated CNL and implement it with the RGL (resource grammar library);
- **top-down**: start with the WCT (wide-coverage translator) and improve it by domain-specific rules (using RGL).

The bottom-up approach was excluded almost immediately, because we had to take the corpus as it was: we had to translate sentences written in different times by different human authors, which could not be expected to follow strict CNL rules.

Figure 2 shows the grammar writing phases. The rectangles are off-the-shelf components from GF open source repositories. The ovals are grammar parts created in the project. The dashed rectangle RGL means that the RGL is used as a library rather than as a part of the run-time translation grammar.

Phase 0: WCT

We started with a baseline using WCT out of the box, just extended with rules for the variables. The results were far from satisfactory. We did receive translations to all sentences, but they were too often relying on robustness (i.e. chunking rather than full analyses), lexical choices were bad, and many words were returned untranslated because they were missing. The same happens with Google translate, because there are many uncommon Swedish words. The grammar at this phase was just the wide-coverage translation grammar of GF.

Phase 1: WCT + lexicon

This phase added the missing words to the lexicon, but the syntax was still the WCT syntax. Many compounds were first translated compositionally from their parts: thus *lekplatsområde* became the incomprehensible *game place section* instead of the correct *playground area*. Such problems could have been partly solved by using the corpus as data for statistical phrase alignment and deriving a GF multiword lexicon from that (Enache et al., 2014). But the data was fully available only for English, and it did not have the desired terminological consistency. Thus we ended up creating a lexicon semiautomatically from the corpus, occasionally adding multiword constructions later when new languages required this. The grammar at this phase was the wide-coverage grammar plus the domain-specific lexicon.

Phase 2: CNL as extended subset of WCT

There were two problems with the grammar built using the top-down strategy:

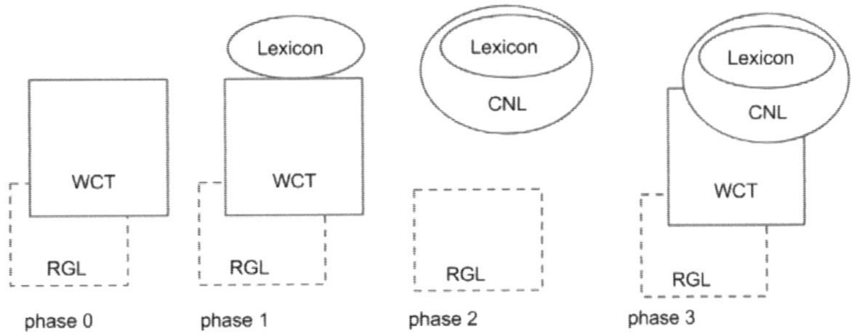

Figure 2: The four phases of grammar development.

- **Ambiguity**: including all syntax rules creates ambiguities that are not adequately solved by the generic statistical model of WCT.
- **Incompleteness**: even though all sentences are parsed, the parses don't capture idiomatic constructions typical of this domain.

The incompleteness concerned not only multiword constructions, but also general syntactic rules. Some authors of the corpus had used a telegraphic style, with missing articles and endings; Swedish expresses definiteness in morphology, for instance, *dörren* = *dörr* + *en* ("the door"). These phenomena required new rules in the general syntax, not just domain-specific CNL rules.

At the same time, only some of the RGL structures turned out to be actually needed. Less than a third of the 216 combination rules in the RGL abstract syntax were used in correct analyses of the corpus; the rest were just creating spurious parses

The module system of GF provides a way to reuse and recombine parts of grammars, even of grammars given as "black boxes" such as the RGL in its standard binary distribution. Using these techniques, we made two kinds of changes on top of the standard RGL:

- **Removing** rules until we got just those parses that made sense for the domain.
- **Adding** rules that enabled parsing input that was not parsed correctly before.

We ended up removing all but 30 rules of the standard RGL and adding about 40 new rules, having to do with the telegraphic style, measument units, and existential constructions. In addition, 16 rules were needed to embed the variables in standard syntactic constructions. They were not always just words, but syntactic functions.

For example, the existential variable `[exist]`, as shown in Figure 1, marks a semantic function that is realized in different ways in different languages. The abstract syntax is simply

```
fun VarExistNPS : NP -> S
```

The linearization has a variable that gets both positive and negative values, "there is/are (not)". This cannot be done by simple slot-filling, because the filler may depend on the surrounding sentence (e.g. "is/are" in English) and because, conversely, the surrounding sentence may depend on the slot filler (in Finnish, the NP is in the nominative if the existential is positive, partitive if negative). However, human translators had been ingenious and found ways to generate acceptable language even with slot filling. Thus the existential verb of Swedish was rendered as an adjective in English (*(not) available*) and in German (*(nicht) erhältlich*). Swedish (*finns (inte)*) and Spanish (*(no) hay*) could both be treated with verbs.

From the engineering point of view, the syntax part was extremely simple. The GF source code is around 180 lines for all languages, as opposed to the lexicon, which is around 1050 lines. The RGL and its common API come with the promise that writing grammars by using the RGL is equally complicated for all languages supported, which is corroborated by these figures; see the full code statistics in Table 2.

The resulting grammar was a CNL based on an abstract syntax that was syntactic rather than semantic. Thus for instance *the length of X is Y* is not parsed as the logical predication `(Length X Y)` but as an NP-VP predication

```
Pred (PossNP X (UseN längd_N))
  (MeasureVP Y)
```

This kind of abstract syntax is also used in ACE (Attempto Controlled English) (Fuchs et al., 2008). The syntactic structures and their logical semantics are known since (Montague, 1974), which makes ACE well suited for inference. But it is not so good for translation, because syntax may have to be changed when going from one language to another. Adding semantic constructions to the abstract syntax would therefore be the way to go if perfect quality was required.

The grammar at this point was a CNL with the lexicon generated in the previous phase, together with a minimal set of syntax rules. This grammar was able to translate 95% of the corpus.

Phase 3: Embedded CNL in WCT

The grammar of phase 2 left 54 sentences unparsed. These sentences were long, tricky, and often ungrammatical. Extending the grammar would have been hard work with diminishing returns. What is more, the time allocated for grammar development was coming to its end. The practical solution was to switch back to the WCT for the remaining sentences.

Since the same grammar was expected to be used later for new sentences, we wanted a solution with the best of both worlds: use CNL as much as possible and WCT only as a back-up. An embedded CNL does this by combining the two grammars under a common start category, say `S_top`. This category can be produced in two ways:

```
UseCNL : S_cnl -> S_top
UseWCT : S_wct -> S_top
```

The weights in the probabilistic parser are set so that `UseCNL` is given priority over `UseWCT`.

However, even unparsed sentences may have parts that belong to the CNL. For instance, they can contain noun phrases that are technical terms whose translation is domain-specific. To make maximal use of these parts, the robust grammar has **coercion rules** from 12 subsentential categories of the CNL to corresponding categories of the WCT, for instance,

```
CoerceNP : NP_cnl -> NP_wct
```

The weights are again set in a way that gives this rule priority over other rules producing `NP_wct`.

The additional grammar module for the robust grammar is just 70 lines, actually the same for all languages except for the import list telling which RGL modules are used. It can therefore be produced automatically for any new language.

The final version of the grammar was now able to parse all sentences in the corpus, 95% with the CNL and 5% with robustness.

5 The translation workflow

With the abstract syntax, Swedish, and English in place, the grammarians of Finnish, German, and Spanish started their work. The Swedish/English grammarian meanwhile produced a treebank covering the whole corpus, to guide the other grammarians. The grammarians used the trees in the treebank to generate their own translations. Figure 3 shows an example entry from the treebank.

The GF translation is often different from the original human translation, either because it is wrong or because it just expresses the meaning in a different way. In Figure 3, both reasons apply. The translation is wrong because it uses the indefinite article; this in turn because the telegraphic Swedish null determiner is rendered as an indefinite in the English grammar - which is correct in most cases, but not in this one (where the omission of determiner in the source is actually a questionable choice). The grammar moreover uses a different word for *gångyta*, namely *walking area* instead of *pedestrian area*. This is fine, because both translations occur in the reference.

The grammarians used the treebank to guide their grammar development. In the last phase, they moved on to just post-editing the translations. The final deliverable of the grammarians was the concrete syntax modules, the machine translations produced by the grammar, and the post-edited correct translations.

6 Evaluation

The first evaluation question is the quality of the translations. Table 1 shows BLEU scores for each language, computed by the Asiya tool (Gonzàlez et al., 2012) by using the post-edited translations as reference, as well as the percentage of translations that were correct without post-editing. The results cover all 1,185 texts of the corpus and are also shown separately for the CNL and robust translations. The Google translate scores are also with a reference obtained by post-editing the MT result minimally. These scores are for a sample of 40 sentences for CNL and 10 for robust translations and hence less representative. Notice that this is not a proper evaluation in the usual sense, because the grammar is tested on the same material that was used for building it; the purpose here is to measure the quality that can be produced by a limited effort, and also to check how it compares to Google translate, which had been previ-

```
Swe: begränsad gångyta är [units] bred
GF:  (Pred (NullDetCN (AdjCN (PastPartA begränsa_V2) (UseN gångyta_N))) (measureVP varMeasure bred_A))
Eng: a restricted walking area is [units] wide
Ref: the limited pedestrian area is [units] wide
```

Figure 3: Example of a GF treebank entry: Swe (source), GF (tree), Eng (GF translation), Ref (human translation).

language	correct	BLEU,GF	Google
Finnish, CNL	48%	**77**	31
Finnish, robust	0%	**31**	20
Finnish, all	46%	**73**	28
German, CNL	44%	**75**	37
German, robust	0%	33	**34**
German, all	42%	**73**	37
Spanish, CNL	34%	**76**	28
Spanish, robust	0%	**39**	25
Spanish, all	32%	**74**	28

Table 1: Quality evaluation.

language	GE	PE	PES	Ws/h	LoC
Finnish	14	6	1200	370	1292
German	18	6	1200	300	1290
Spanish	38	8	900	160	1291
Swedish	12	-	-	-	1303
English	12	-	-	-	1284
abstract	12	-	-	-	1286
prepare	12	-	-	-	400
total	118	20	1100	160	8056

Table 2: The grammar writing and translation effort. GE = grammar engineering (hours), PE = postediting (hours), PES Ws (post-editing speed words per hour), Ws/h (words translated per hour of work), LoC = lines of GF/Haskell code. The "total" for PES and Ws/h means the average of all languages.

ously used by the customer.

The second evaluation question is the productivity of grammar writing as a translation method. Table 2 shows the working hours and lines of GF code spent on different languages. The "prepare" score shows the hours spent on analysing and preparing the data and the amount of Haskell code written to help the task. The main result is that the time budget was held: 200 hours were allocated and 138 used. The high post-edit speed predicts that system development costs are amortized as more texts are translated. The time difference between the Spanish and other grammarians reflects the prior GF expertise of the grammarians and also the availability of some prior Finnish and German translations that helped with the technical terminology. Each new language amortizes the cost of the generic parts (48 hours), due to the interlingual architecture. The interlingual RGL explains why different languages need similar amounts of GF code.

7 Related work

Grammar-based translation is familiar from compilers, where synchronous grammars (Aho and Ullman, 1969) are a technique that has also been applied to human languages. With its explicit interlingua (abstract syntax), GF resembles (Rosetta, 1994), whereas most other approaches are based on transfer, e.g. (Rayner et al., 2000; Butt et al., 2002; Rayner et al., 2006).

The quality of the earlier GF projects using pure CNLs is higher, with typical BLEU scores between 80 and 95 (Rautio and Koponen, 2013). But it is interesting to note that even in those cases, the post-editors were not fully satisfied. Thus it is not clear if translation can be made completely automatic, if dissemination quality is the goal.

8 Conclusion

How to best build a system like this? The embedded CNL approach provided a good balance of quality and robustness. The CNL parsed 95% of the sentences, and covering the rest would have given diminishing returns. Including more semantic constructions (rather than syntactic combinations) in the CNL could have given better quality.

How good is the quality? The BLEU scores were at least 73 for all languages, which meant easy post-editing, at least 900 words per hour.

Is this approach commercially viable? The translation of the corpus to three languages was made at the rate of 160 words per hour, which includes both grammar writing and post-editing. This is comparable to human translation, so that we are just above the bar if only this corpus is considered. However, the high post-editing speed suggests that building grammars is profitable if more text of the same kind is translated later. Moreover, the interlingual architecture of GF enables new languages to be added at lower costs.

References

Alfred V. Aho and Jeffrey D. Ullman. 1969. Syntax directed translations and the pushdown assembler. *Journal of Computer and System Sciences*, 3(1):37 – 56.

Krasimir Angelov and Peter Ljunglöf. 2014. Fast statistical parsing with parallel multiple context-free grammars. In *EACL'14*, pages 368–376.

Krasimir Angelov, Björn Bringert, and Aarne Ranta. 2014. Speech-enabled hybrid multilingual translation for mobile devices. *EACL'14*, pages 41–44.

Lars Borin, Markus Forsberg, and Lennart Lönngren. 2013. Saldo: a touch of yin to wordnet's yang. *Language resources and evaluation*, 47(4):1191–1211.

Miriam Butt, Helge Dyvik, Tracy Holloway King, Hiroshi Masuichi, and Christian Rohrer. 2002. The parallel grammar project. In *Proceedings of the 2002 workshop on Grammar engineering and evaluation-Volume 15*, pages 1–7. Association for Computational Linguistics.

Haskell B. Curry. 1961. Some logical aspects of grammatical structure. In Roman Jakobson, editor, *Structure of Language and its Mathematical Aspects: Proceedings of the Twelfth Symposium in Applied Mathematics*, pages 56–68. American Mathematical Society.

Mariana Damova, Dana Dannélls, Ramona Enache, Maria Mateva, and Aarne Ranta. 2014. Multilingual natural language interaction with semantic web knowledge bases and linked open data. In *Towards the Multilingual Semantic Web*, pages 211–226. Springer Berlin Heidelberg.

Brian Davis, Ramona Enache, Jeroen van Grondelle, and Laurette Pretorius. 2012. Multilingual verbalisation of modular ontologies using gf and lemon. In Tobias Kuhn and Norbert Fuchs, editors, *Controlled Natural Language*, volume 7427 of *LNCS/LNAI*, pages 167–184. Springer.

Grégoire Détrez and Aarne Ranta. 2012. Smart paradigms and the predictability and complexity of inflectional morphology. In *EACL (European Association for Computational Linguistics)*, Avignon, April. Association for Computational Linguistics.

Marc Dymetman, Veronika Lux, and Aarne Ranta. 2000. XML and multilingual document authoring: Convergent trends. In *Proc. Computational Linguistics COLING, Saarbrücken, Germany*, pages 243–249. International Committee on Computational Linguistics.

Ramona Enache, Inari Listenmaa, and Prasanth Kolachina. 2014. Handling non-compositionality in multilingual CNLs. In *Controlled Natural Language - 4th International Workshop, CNL 2014, Galway, Ireland, August 20-22, 2014. Proceedings*, volume 8625 of *LNCS*.

Norbert E. Fuchs, Kaarel Kaljurand, and Tobias Kuhn. 2008. Attempto Controlled English for Knowledge Representation. In Cristina Baroglio, Piero A. Bonatti, Jan Małuszyński, Massimo Marchiori, Axel Polleres, and Sebastian Schaffert, editors, *Reasoning Web, Fourth International Summer School 2008*, number 5224 in LNCS, pages 104–124. Springer.

Meritxell Gonzàlez, Jesús Giménez, and Lluís Màrquez. 2012. A Graphical Interface for MT Evaluation and Error Analysis. In *The 50th Annual Meeting of the Association for Computational Linguistics*.

Thomas Hallgren, Aarne Ranta, John Camilleri, Grégoire Détrez, and Ramona Enache. 2012. Grammar Tools and Best Practices. MOLTO Deliverable D2.3, June.

Richard Montague. 1974. *Formal Philosophy*. Yale University Press, New Haven. Collected papers edited by Richmond Thomason.

Aarne Ranta, Ramona Enache, and Grégoire Détrez. 2012. Controlled Language for Everyday Use: the MOLTO Phrasebook. In Tobias Kuhn and Norbert Fuchs, editors, *Controlled Natural Language*, volume 7427 of *LNCS/LNAI*. Springer.

Aarne Ranta. 2009. The GF Resource Grammar Library. *Linguistics in Language Technology*, 2:1–65.

Aarne Ranta. 2011. *Grammatical Framework: Programming with Multilingual Grammars*. CSLI Publications, Stanford.

Aarne Ranta. 2014. Embedded controlled languages. In *Controlled Natural Language - 4th International Workshop, CNL 2014, Galway, Ireland, August 20-22, 2014. Proceedings*, volume 8625 of *LNCS*.

Jussi Rautio and Maarit Koponen. 2013. Deliverable 9.2: Molto evaluation and assessment report.

Manny Rayner, David Carter, Pierrette Bouillon, Vassilis Digalakis, and Mats Wirén. 2000. *The Spoken Language Translator*. Cambridge University Press, Cambridge.

Manny Rayner, Beth Ann Hockey, and Pierrette Bouillon. 2006. *Putting Linguistics into Speech Recognition: The Regulus Grammar Compiler*. CSLI Publications.

M. T. Rosetta. 1994. *Compositional Translation*. Kluwer, Dordrecht.

Jordi Saludes and Sebastian Xambó. 2011. The gf mathematics library. In Pedro Quaresma and Ralph-Johan Back, editors, *Proceedings First Workshop on CTP Components for Educational Software (THedu'11)*, number 79, pages 102–110. Electronic Proceedings in Theoretical Computer Science, 02/2012.

Building an HPSG-based Indonesian Resource Grammar (INDRA)

David Moeljadi **Francis Bond** **Sanghoun Song**
Division of Linguistics and Multilingual Studies
Nanyang Technological University
Singapore
{D001,fcbond,sanghoun}@ntu.edu.sg

Abstract

This paper presents the creation and the initial stage development of a broad-coverage Indonesian Resource Grammar (INDRA) within the framework of Head Driven Phrase Structure Grammar (HPSG) (Pollard and Sag, 1994) and Minimal Recursion Semantics (MRS) (Copestake et al., 2005). At the present stage, INDRA focuses on verbal constructions and subcategorization since they are fundamental for argument and event structure. Verbs in INDRA were semi-automatically acquired from the English Resource Grammar (ERG) (Flickinger, 2000) via Wordnet Bahasa (Nurril Hirfana Mohamed Noor et al., 2011; Bond et al., 2014). In the future, INDRA will be used in the development process of machine translation. A preliminary evaluation of INDRA on the MRS test-suite shows promising coverage.

1 Introduction to Indonesian

Indonesian (ISO 639-3: ind) is a Western Malayo-Polynesian language of the Austronesian language family. Within this subgroup, it belongs to the Malayic branch with Standard Malay in Malaysia and other Malay varieties (Lewis, 2009). It is spoken mainly in the Republic of Indonesia as the sole official and national language and as the common language for hundreds of ethnic groups living there (Alwi et al., 2014, pp. 1-2). In Indonesia it is spoken by around 22.8 million people as their first language and by more than 140 million people as their second language. The lexical similarity is over 80% with Standard Malay (Lewis, 2009).

Morphologically, Indonesian is a mildly agglutinative language, compared to Finnish or Turkish where the morpheme-per-word ratio is higher (Larasati et al., 2011). It has a rich affixation system, including a variety of prefixes, suffixes, circumfixes, and reduplication. Most of the affixes are derivational. Two important inflectional affixes are the prefix *meN-* which marks active voice and *di-* which denotes passive voice (Sneddon et al., 2010, pp. 29, 72).

Indonesian has a strong tendency to be head-initial (Sneddon et al., 2010, pp. 26-28). In a noun phrase with an adjective, a demonstrative or a relative clause, the head noun precedes the adjective, the demonstrative or the relative clause. There is no agreement in Indonesian. In general, grammatical relations are only distinguished in terms of word order. As is often the case with Austronesian languages of Indonesia, Indonesian has a basic word order of SVO with a nominative-accusative alignment pattern. Argument alternations are triggered by passive and applicative constructions.

2 Background

This section introduces the background theory, as well as an overview of the Deep Linguistic Processing with HPSG Initiative (DELPH-IN) and the tools to build and develop INDRA.

2.1 Frameworks

INDRA uses the theoretical framework of HPSG (Pollard and Sag, 1994). HPSG is monostratal, handling orthography, syntax, semantics and pragmatics in a single structure (sign), modeled through typed feature structures. HPSG is unification- and constraint-based. The words and phrases are combined according to constraints of the lexical entries based on the type hierarchy. INDRA uses MRS (Copestake et al., 2005) as its semantic framework because it is adaptable for HPSG typed-feature structure and suitable for parsing and generation. The semantic structures in MRS are underspecified for scope and thus suitable for representing ambiguous scoping.

Proceedings of the Grammar Engineering Across Frameworks (GEAF) Workshop, 53rd Annual Meeting of the ACL and 7th IJCNLP, pages 9–16,
Beijing, China, July 26-31, 2015. ©2015 Association for Computational Linguistics

There is no previous work done on Indonesian HPSG but much has been done using Lexical Functional Grammar (LFG) (Kaplan and Bresnan, 1982), e.g. Arka and Manning (2008) on active and passive voice and Arka (2000) on control constructions. In addition, Arka (2012) and Mistica (2013) have worked on the computational grammar "IndoGram" which is a part of the ParGram (Sulger et al., 2013).[1] However, it is not open-source or very broad in its coverage. Further, it does not produce MRS, so cannot be easily incorporated into our machine translation system. Thus, there is a need to build and develop a broad-coverage open-source HPSG of Indonesian.

2.2 DELPH-IN

The DELPH-IN consortium (Deep Linguistic Processing with HPSG Initiative, `http://www.delph-in.net`) is a research collaboration between linguists and computer scientists which builds and develops open source grammar, tools for grammar development and applications using HPSG and MRS. More than fifteen grammars have been created and developed within DELPH-IN, e.g. English Resource Grammar (ERG) (Copestake and Flickinger, 2000) and Japanese grammar Jacy (Siegel and Bender, 2002). DELPH-IN grammars define typed feature structures using Type Description Language (TDL) (Copestake, 2002).

We make extensive use of several open-source tools for grammar development provided by DELPH-IN: Linguistic Knowledge Builder (LKB) (Copestake, 2002), a grammar and lexicon development environment for typed feature structure grammars; The LinGO Grammar Matrix (Bender et al., 2010), a web-based questionnaire for writing new DELPH-IN grammars, providing a wide range of phenomena and basic files to make the grammars compatible with DELPH-IN parsers and generators; Answer Constraint Engine (ACE) (`http://sweaglesw.org/linguistics/ace/`), an efficient processor for DELPH-IN grammars; ITSDB or [incr tsdb()] (Oepen and Flickinger, 1998), a tool for testing, profiling the performance of the grammar and treebanking; Full Forest Treebanker (FFTB) (`http://moin.delph-in.net/FftbTop`), a treebanking tool for DELPH-IN grammars, allowing the selection of an arbitrary tree from the "full forest" without enumerating all analyses in the parsing stage; and LOGON (Oepen et al., 2007), a collection of software, grammars, and other linguistic resources for transfer-based machine translation.

[1] `http://iness.uib.no/iness/xle-web`

3 INDRA

This section describes some preliminary work as well as the methodology.

3.1 Methodology

The methodology used in INDRA follows Bender et al. (2008). We model our analysis in HPSG and implement it by editing some TDL files after analyzing a phenomenon based on reference grammars and other linguistic literatures. Afterwards, we compile the grammar and test it by parsing sample sentences or test-suites. The grammar is debugged and developed further if some gaps or problems are found according to the parse results. Afterwards, the sample sentences in test-suites will be parsed again and treebanked. This process goes repetitively. If problems are not found or the debugging process has finished with a good result, the grammar will be updated in GitHub (`https://github.com/davidmoeljadi/INDRA`).

3.2 Grammar Development

INDRA was created firstly by filling in the required sections of the online page of LinGO Grammar Matrix questionnaire which covers basic grammar phenomena such as word order, tense-aspect-mode, coordination, morphology, subcategorization of nouns and verbs (`http://www.delph-in.net/matrix/customize/matrix.cgi`). INDRA subcategorizes nouns into three groups: common noun, pronoun and proper name. Common nouns are subcategorized into inanimate, non-human and human based on three main classifiers in Indonesian: the classifier *buah* (lit. fruit) for inanimate nouns, *ekor* (lit. tail) for non-human animate nouns and *orang* (lit. person) for human nouns (Sneddon et al., 2010, p. 139; Alwi et al., 2014, p. 288).

Verbs are subcategorized into three groups: intransitive which has one argument, transitive which has two arguments and optional transitive which has one obligatory subject argument and one optional object argument as in *Adi makan (nasi)* "Adi eats (rice)". The verb subcategorization here follows Alwi et al. (2014, pp. 95-98). Besides the number of arguments, the possibility of passivization with morphological inflection plays an important role in distinguishing intransitives from transitives in Indonesian. Examples [1] and [2a] show intransitive and transitive sentences respectively.

(1) *Adi tidur.*
Adi sleep
"Adi sleeps."

(2) a. *Adi mengejar Budi.*
Adi ACT-chase Budi
"Adi chases Budi."

b. *Budi dikejar Adi.*
Budi PASS-chase Adi
"Budi is chased by Adi."

c. *Budi saya kejar.*
Budi 1SG chase
"Budi is chased by me."

In Example (2a), the verb *mengejar* is formed from an active prefix *meN-* and the base *kejar* (the initial sound *k* undergoes nasalization; see Section 4.2). The active prefix *meN-* is changed to a passive prefix *di-* in passive type one (Sneddon et al., 2010, pp. 256-257) in Example (2b) and without affix in passive type two (Sneddon et al., 2010, pp. 257-258) in Example (2c). Sneddon et al. (2010, pp. 256-257) states that in passive type one, the actor is third person or a noun, while in passive two, the agent is a pronoun or pronoun substitute and it comes before the unprefixed verb.

The more detailed verb subcategorization into other groups such as ditransitive will be mentioned in the next subsection. The lexical items for each noun and verb subcategory were added and the affixes to support the active-passive voice were included. However, the Matrix does not handle morphology as in the nasalization process of *meN-* and thus has to be manually added (see Section 4.2).

3.3 Lexical Acquisition

The lexicon is important in the robustness of the grammar. Since inputting words or lexical entries manually into the grammar is labor intensive and time consuming, doing lexical acquisition semi-automatically is vital. In order to do this, we need good lexical resources. We attempted to extract Indonesian verbs from Wordnet Bahasa (Nurril Hirfana Mohamed Noor et al., 2011; Bond et al., 2014) and group them based on syntactic types in the ERG, such as intransitive, transitive, and ditransitive, using Python 3.4 and Natural Language Toolkit (NLTK) (Bird et al., 2009). The grouping of verbs (verb frames) in Wordnet (Fellbaum, 1998) is employed to be the bridge between the English and Indonesian grammar.

Each verb synset in Wordnet (also Wordnet Bahasa) contains a list of sentence frames specified by the lexicographer illustrating the types of simple sentences in which the verbs in the synset can be used (Fellbaum, 1998). There are 35 verbal sentence frames in Wordnet, some of them are shown as follows with their frame numbers:

(3) 1 Something ----s
8 Somebody ----s something
21 Somebody ----s something PP

Frame 1 is a typical intransitive verbal sentence frame, as in *the book fell*; frame 8 is a typical (mono)transitive verbal sentence frame, as in *he chases his friend*; and frame 21 is a typical ditransitive verbal sentence frame, as in *she put a book on a table*. A verb may have more than one synset and each synset may have more than one verb frame, e.g. the verb *eat* has six synsets with each synset having different verb frames. Three of the six synsets, together with their definition and verb frames, are presented in Table 1. These verb frames can be employed as a bridge between the verb types (also verb lexical items) in ERG and those in INDRA.

Synset	Definition	Verb frame
01168468-v	Take in solid food	8 Somebody ----s something
01166351-v	Eat a meal, take a meal	2 Somebody ----s
01157517-v	Use up (resources or materials)	11 Something ----s something 8 Somebody ----s something

Table 1: Three of six synsets of the verb "eat" and their verb frames in Wordnet

Out of 354 verb types in ERG, the top eleven most frequently used types in the corpus were chosen, excluding the specific English verb types such as *be*-type verbs (e.g. *is*, *be* and *was*), *have*-type verbs, verbs with prepositions (e.g. *depend on*, *refer to* and *look after*) and modals (e.g. *would*, *may* and *need*). The chosen eleven verb types are given in Table 2. The third, fifth and eighth type (*v_-_unacc_le*, *v_-_le* and *v_pp_unacc_le* all written in bold in Table 2) are regarded as the same type, i.e. intransitive verb type, in INDRA.

Verb type	Freq		Examples of verb
	Corp	Lex	
v_pp*_dir_le	7079	204	go, come, hike
v_vp_seq_le	3921	105	want, like, try
_-_unacc_le	3144	334	close, start, end
v_np_noarg3_le	2723	5	make, take, give
v_-_le	2666	486	arrive, occur, stand
v_np-pp_e_le	2439	334	compare, know, relate
v_pp*-cp_le	2360	154	think, add, note
v_pp_unacc_le	2307	44	rise, fall, grow
v_np-pp_prop_le	1861	135	base, put, locate
v_cp_prop_le	1600	80	believe, know, find
v_np_ntr_le	1558	10	get, want, total

Table 2: The ten most frequently used ERG verb types in the corpus

The first type contains verbs expressing movement or direction with optional PP complements, as in *B crept into the room*. The verbs in the second type are subject control verbs, as in *B intended to win*. The third type consists of unaccusative verbs without complements as in *The plate gleamed*. The fourth type contains verbs having two arguments (monotransitive) although they have a potential to be ditransitive as in *B took the book*. The fifth type contains intransitive (unergative) verbs as in *B arose*. The verbs in the sixth type have obligatory NP and PP complements as in *B compared C with D*. The verbs in the seventh type are verbs with optional PP complements and obligatory subordinate clauses as in *B said to C that D won*. Unaccusative verbs with optional PP complements as in *The seed grew into a tree* belong to the eighth type. Ditransitive verbs with obligatory NPs and PPs with state result as in *B put C on D* belong to the ninth type. The tenth type consists of verbs with optional complementizers as in *B hoped (that) C won* and the eleventh type consists of verbs with obligatory NP complements which cannot be passivized as in *B remains C*.

Based on the syntactic information of each verb type mentioned above, the corresponding verb frames in Wordnet were manually chosen. For example, the first type contains intransitive verbs with optional PP; thus, the verb frames should be Sb ----s and Sb ----s PP. The intransitive verbs without complements should correspond to the verb frames Sth ----s or Sb ----s, regardless of whether the subject is a thing or a person. Table 3 shows the eleven verb types in ERG and their corresponding Wordnet verb frames.

First, we checked for each verb in each verb

Verb type	Verb frame
v_pp*_dir_le	2 Sb ----s & 22 Sb ----s PP
v_vp_seq_le	28 Sb ----s to INFINITIVE
v_-_unacc_le v_-_le v_pp_unacc_le	1 Sth ----s || 2 Sb ----s
v_np_noarg3_le	8 Sb ----s sth || 11 Sth ----s sth
v_np-pp_e_le	15 Sb ----s sth to sb || 17 Sb ----s sb with sth || 20 Sb ----s sb PP || 21 Sb ----s sth PP || 31 Sb ----s sth with sth
v_pp*-cp_le	26 Sb ----s that CLAUSE
v_np-pp_prop_le	20 Sb ----s sb PP || 21 Sb ----s sth PP
v_cp_prop_le	26 Sb ----s that CLAUSE
v_np_ntr_le	8 Sb ----s sth || 11 Sth ----s sth

Table 3: The eleven most frequently used ERG verb types in the corpus and their corresponding Wordnet verb frames (sb = somebody, sth = something, & = AND, || = OR

type in Table 2 whether it is in Wordnet or not. If it could be found in Wordnet, the next step was to check whether the verb includes the verb frames mentioned in Table 3 or not. This step had to be done in order to find out the right synset since a verb can have many synsets but different verb frames as shown in Table 1. After the right synset was found, the corresponding Indonesian lemmas or translations were checked. One synset may have more than one Indonesian lemma or may not have Indonesian lemmas at all.

The next important step is to check one by one the Indonesian lemmas belonging to the same synset and verb frames whether each can be grouped in the same verb type or not. This manual step has to be done because grouping verbs in a particular language into types is a language-specific work. Arka (2000) states that languages vary with respect to their lexical stock of "synonymous" verbs that may have different argument structures, e.g. the verb *know* can be both intransitive and transitive in Indonesian *tahu* and *ketahui* respectively, transitive only with an obligatory NP in Balinese[2] *tawang*, and transitive with optional NP in English *know*. Lastly, after the Indonesian verbs were extracted and grouped into their cor-

[2]Balinese (ISO 639-3: ban) is a Western Malayo-Polynesian language of the Austronesian language family. It belongs to the Malayo-Sumbawan branch. It is mainly spoken in the island of Bali in the Republic of Indonesia as a regional language (Lewis, 2009).

responding verb types, a new lexicon file for INDRA was made, in which the verbs are alphabetically sorted. The result is, in total, 939 Indonesian verbs were extracted and grouped into nine verb types as presented in Table 4. One verb may belong to more than one verb type.

This lexical acquisition is useful to extract lexical items (semi-)automatically through linguistic resources such as Wordnet Bahasa. The generated lexicon can be used to improve the grammar's coverage. We plan to further extract more verbs as well as other parts-of-speech such as nouns, adjectives and adverbs.

Verb type	Number of verb
v_pp*_dir_le	76
v_vp_seq_le	49
v_-_unacc_le	594
v_np_noarg3_le	5
v_np-pp_e_le	41
v_pp*-cp_le	23
v_np-pp_prop_le	85
v_cp_prop_le	53
v_np_ntr_le	13
Total	939

Table 4: New verb types and the corresponding number of verbs in INDRA

4 Analyzing Indonesian Phenomena

After creating INDRA via the Grammar Matrix customization system, some additions and changes were done to the TDL files. Pronouns, proper names and adjectives which were formerly added via the Grammar Matrix customization system, were subsequently constrained so that they cannot parse phrases such as **saya kaya* "rich I". In addition, besides the new verb types which had been acquired from ERG, more verb rules such as control and raising were manually added. In total, there are 49 lexical types/categories in the lexicon.

The next subsections discuss some phenomena, e.g. decomposing words and morphology, analyzed and implemented in INDRA.

4.1 Decomposed Words

Following Seah and Bond (2014) who state that pronouns can be analyzed componentially, some words such as *sini* "here" can be mapped to multiple predicates, e.g. *sini* "here" can be thought of as *tempat ini* "this place". The way to model this is by defining type hierarchies for the head (e.g. *tempat* "place") and the demonstrative (e.g. *ini* "this"). Figure 1 and 2 show the type hierarchy for heads and demonstratives respectively.

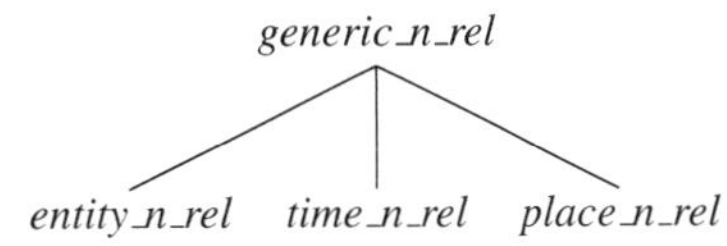

Figure 1: Type hierarchy for heads

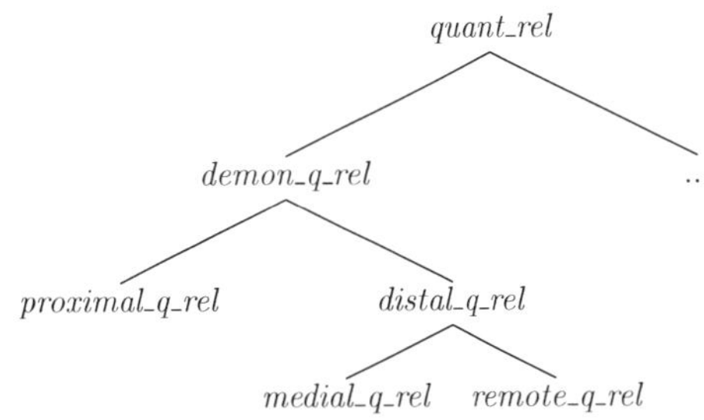

Figure 2: Type hierarchy for demonstratives

Indonesian has two demonstratives: *ini* "this" and *itu* "that" but three locative pronouns: *sini* "here (near speaker)", *situ* "there (not far off)" and *sana* "there (far off)" (Sneddon et al., 2010, pp. 133, 195). These can be modeled using the type hierarchy for demonstratives. The demonstrative *itu* "that" has the predicate *distal_q_rel*; the locative pronouns *situ* and *sana* has the predicate *medial_q_rel* and *remote_q_rel* respectively, which are the daughters of the predicate *distal_q_rel*. Figure 3 shows the implementation in TDL.

Figure 4 shows the MRS representation of the decomposed word *situ* "there" which is preceded by a preposition *di* "at". The ARG0 in the semantic head daughter *di* "at" is equated with the INDEX which has the value *e*2. The value of the ARG2 (*x*4) is coindexed with the ARG0 of *place_n_rel* and *medial_q_rel*. The *medial_q_rel* introduces RSTR which is related to the top handle of the quantifier's restriction (*h*7) and linked to the LBL of *place_n_rel* ($h7 =_q h5$).

Decomposing words is important to get more refined semantics. We will expand this to other heads and demonstratives such as *kini* "at present" which can be decomposed into *time_n_rel* and

```
situ := n+det-lex &
 [STEM < "situ" >,
  SYNSEM.LKEYS [ KEYREL.PRED "place_n_rel",
                 ALTKEYREL.PRED "medial_q_rel"]].
```

Figure 3: Decomposed predicates of *situ* "there"

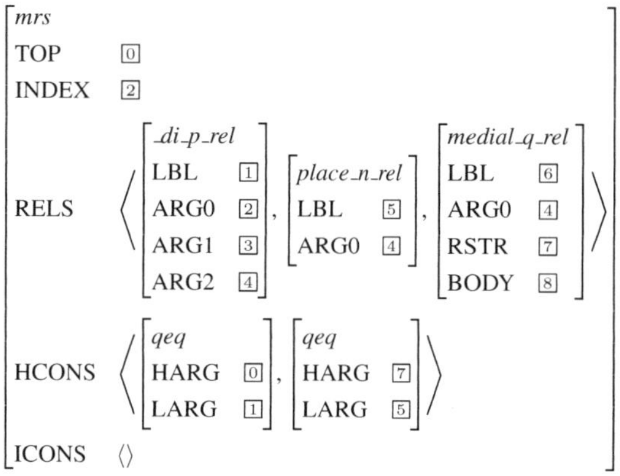

Figure 4: MRS representation of *di situ* (lit. "at there")

proximal_q_rel.

4.2 Morphology

As mentioned in Section 3.2, a number of nasalization (sound changes) or morphology process occur when *meN-* combines with bases. Table 5 shows us that a number of sound changes occur when *meN-* combines with a base. A base loses its initial consonant if the consonant is one of the following voiceless consonants: *p*, *t*, *s* and *k*. It retains its initial consonant otherwise. The sound changes of every possible combination of consonant clusters in Alwi et al. (2014, pp. 67-68) was manually examined using an online Indonsian dictionary (KBBI Daring) (Alwi et al., 2008). In addition, when the base consists of only one syllable, *meN-* becomes *menge-* with no sound changes in the base. Every possible combination of one syllable word with *meN-* which forms a transitive verb in KBBI Daring was listed up. There were 44 one syllable words in total. All 24 possible consonant clusters and 44 one syllable words were added to the inflectional rules in INDRA.

Moreover, besides the consonant clusters and one syllable words, a manual extension was also done for the exceptions. The sound *p* is usually lost when combined with *meN-* but it is retained when it is a derivational prefix *per-* as in *pertinggi* (from *per-* and *tinggi* "high"). At the present stage, all transitive bases with *per-* are being listed up and will be added in INDRA. There are also bases such as *punyai* "have" and *syairkan* "compose a poem" (Sneddon et al., 2010, pp. 16-17) which do not undergo the common sound changes.

At the present stage, this morphology process

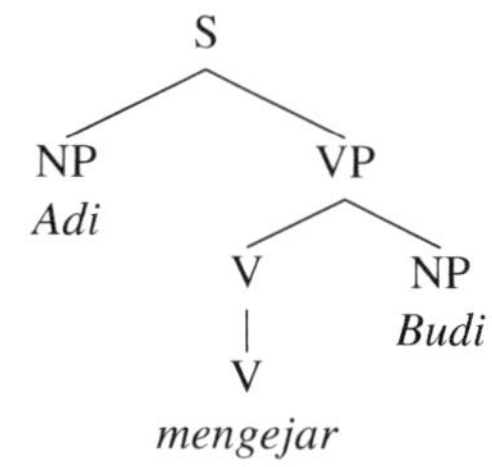

Figure 5: Parse tree of *Adi mengejar Budi* "Adi chases Budi"

applies to all transitive verbs in INDRA with a constraint stating that objects are obligatory. Other verb types such as ditransitives, control and raising which can be passivized will be further included in the inflectional rules. At present, INDRA can parse the example (2a) as shown in Figure 5. The MRS representation is exactly the same as the MRS representation for transitive sentences (see Figure 6). The value of `ARG0` of the semantic head daughter *_kejar_v_rel* is an event (*e*2) which is equated with the `INDEX`. The value of `ARG0` of *named_rel "adi"* (*x*3) and *named_rel "budi"* (*x*9) refer to the value of the `ARG1` and `ARG2` feature of the semantic head daughter respectively.

We intend to cover all the exceptions in the inflectional rules, particularly dealing with words having *per-* and to expand the rules to other verb types such as ditransitives. Passive type one and type two rules also need to be analyzed and implemented. As Sneddon et al. (2010, pp. 256, 263-264) pointed out, passive constructions in Indonesian are far more frequent than in English; an Indonesian passive is often naturally translated into English by an active construction. Thus, dealing with passive constructions will increase the grammar coverage. We anticipate that translating Indonesian passive constructions into English will be a challenge for machine translation.

5 Associated Resources

In order to make INDRA more robust, the following resources have been set up: Indonesian POS Tagger (Rashel et al., 2014) with ACE's YY-mode for unknown word handling (`http://moin.delph-in.net/ZhongYYMode`) which can parse sentences with unknown words and transfer grammar for machine translation. At present, INDRA can translate some simple sentences such as the ones in example (1) and (2a) using the `inen` (Indonesian-English) transfer grammar.

Allomorph of *meN-*	Initial orthography of the base		Example
mem-	p	(L)	*me**m~~p~~**akai* "use"
	pl, pr, ps, pt, b, bl, br, f, fl, fr, v	(R)	*me**mb**eli* "buy"
men-	t	(L)	*me**n~~t~~**anam* "plant"
	tr, ts, d, dr, c, j, sl, sr, sy, sw, sp, st, sk, sm, sn, z	(R)	*me**nc**ari* "seek"
meny-	s	(L)	*me**ny~~s~~**ewa* "rent"
meng-	k	(L)	*me**ng~~k~~**irim* "send"
	kh, kl, kr, g, gl, gr, h, q, a, i, u, e, o	(R)	*me**ngg**anti* "replace"
me-	m, n, ny, ng, l, r, w, y	(R)	*me**l**empar* "throw"
menge-	(base with one syllable)		*me**ngecek*** "check"

Table 5: Morphology process of *meN-* (L = lost, R = retained; Sneddon et al., 2010: 13-18)

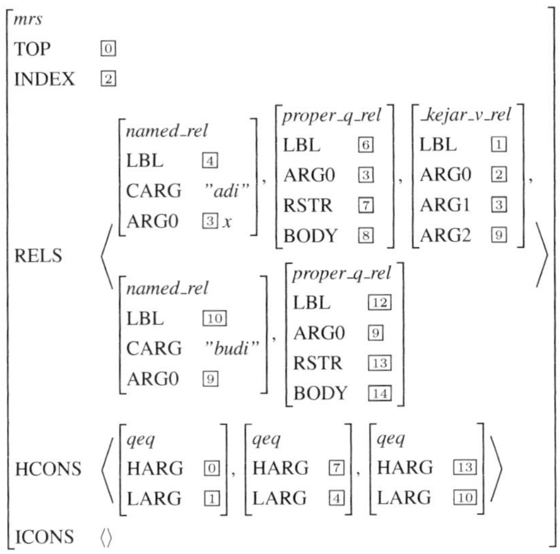

Figure 6: MRS representation of *Adi mengejar Budi* "Adi chases Budi"

6 Evaluation

A test-suite designed to show various semantic phenomena for Indonesian (MRS test-suite) was created based on the original set of 107 sentences in English. The [incr tsdb()] tool (Oepen and Flickinger, 1998) is employed for grammar testing and profiling. Out of 172 sentences, INDRA can parse 55 of them (overall coverage 32%). We got this 32% coverage after the lexical acquisition described in Section 3.3. Table 6 shows the coverage before and after lexical acquisition.

As of 18 June 2015, INDRA contains 1,235 lexical items, 939 of which are verbs extracted from ERG via Wordnet Bahasa; 6 lexical rules; 20 grammar rules; 135 features and 1,596 types. In addition to the phenomena in the Grammar Matrix customization system, INDRA also covers proper names, definiteness, possessive enclitics, adverbs, control and raising, decomposed words and morphology. Phenomena which are planned to be covered in the next two years are relative clauses, numbers, quantifiers, classifiers, copula constructions, passives, topic-comment constructions, particles, interrogatives and imperatives. We estimate that 15% of the MRS test-suite would be covered once passives and relative clauses were added.

	results / items	coverage
before	52 / 172	30.2%
after	55 / 172	32.0%

Table 6: Comparison of coverage in MRS test-suite before and after lexical acquisition

7 Summary and Future Work

The lexical acquisition has proved that by acquiring more lexical items, the grammar's coverage can be improved. We plan to do more lexical acquisition for verbs, nouns, adjectives and adverbs in the future. At the same time, lexical types, rules and constraints for new lexical items will be added. Our plan in the next two years is to cover at least 60% of Indonesian text in the Nanyang Technological University — Multilingual Corpus (NTU-MC) (Tan and Bond, 2012). The latest version of INDRA is regularly backed up in GitHub.

Acknowledgments

Thanks to Michael Wayne Goodman and Dan Flickinger for teaching us how to use GitHub and FFTB. Thanks to Fam Rashel for helping us with POS Tagger and to Lian Tze Lim for helping us improve Wordnet Bahasa. This research was supported in part by the MOE Tier 2 grant *That's what you meant: a Rich Representation for Manipulation of Meaning* (MOE ARC41/13).

References

Hasan Alwi, Dendy Sugono, and Sri Sukesi Adiwimarta. 2008. *Kamus Besar Bahasa Indonesia Dalam Jaringan (KBBI Daring)*. 3 edition.

Hasan Alwi, Soenjono Dardjowidjojo, Hans Lapoliwa, and Anton M. Moeliono. 2014. *Tata Bahasa Baku Bahasa Indonesia*. Balai Pustaka, Jakarta, 3 edition.

I Wayan Arka and C. D. Manning. 2008. Voice and grammatical relations in Indonesian: a new perspective. In *Voice and Grammatical Relations in Austronesian Languages*, pages 45–69. CSLI Publications, Stanford.

I Wayan Arka. 2000. Control and argument structure: explaining control into subject in Indonesian. In *Fourth International Symposium on Malay/Indonesian Linguistics*, Jakarta.

I Wayan Arka. 2012. Developing a deep grammar of indonesian within the pargram framework: Theoretical and implementational challenges. In *26th Pacific Asia Conference on Language, Information and Computation*, pages 19–38.

Emily M Bender, Dan Flickinger, and Stephan Oepen. 2008. Grammar engineering for linguistic hypothesis testing. In *Proceedings of the Texas Linguistics Society X conference: Computational linguistics for less-studied languages*, pages 16–36.

Emily M. Bender, Scott Drellishak, Antske Fokkens, Laurie Poulson, and Safiyyah Saleem. 2010. Grammar customization. In *Research on Language and Computation*, pages 23–72. Springer, Netherlands.

Steven Bird, Edward Loper, and Ewan Klein. 2009. *Natural Language Processing with Python*. O'Reilly Media Inc.

Francis Bond, Lian Tze Lim, Enya Kong Tang, and Hammam Riza. 2014. The combined wordnet bahasa. *NUSA: Linguistic studies of languages in and around Indonesia*, 57:83–100.

Ann Copestake and Dan Flickinger. 2000. An open-source grammar development environment and broad-coverage English grammar using HPSG. In *Proceedings of the Second Conference on Language Resources and Evaluation (LREC-2000)*, Athens.

Ann Copestake, Dan Flickinger, Carl Pollard, and Ivan A. Sag. 2005. Minimal Recursion Semantics: An Introduction. *Research on Language and Computation*, 3(4):281–332.

Ann Copestake. 2002. *Implementing Typed Feature Structure Grammars*. CSLI Publications, Stanford.

Christiane Fellbaum. 1998. *WordNet: an electronic lexical database*. MIT Press, Cambridge.

Dan Flickinger. 2000. On Building a More Efficient Grammar by Exploiting Types. 6(1):15–28.

Ronald Kaplan and Joan Bresnan. 1982. Lexical Functional Grammar: A formal system for grammatical representation. In *The Mental Representation of Grammatical Relations*, pages 173–281. the MIT Press, Cambridge.

Septina Dian Larasati, Vladislav Kuboň, and Daniel Zeman. 2011. Indonesian Morphology Tool (MorphInd): Towards an Indonesian Corpus. *Springer CCIS proceedings of the Workshop on Systems and Frameworks for Computational Morphology*, pages 119–129, August.

M. Paul Lewis. 2009. *Ethnologue: Languages of the World*. SIL International, Dallas, Texas, 16 edition.

Meladel Mistica. 2013. *An Investigation into Deviant Morphology: Issues in the Implementation of a Deep Grammar for Indonesian*. PhD dissertation, The Australian National University, Canberra.

Nurril Hirfana Mohamed Noor, Suerya Sapuan, and Francis Bond. 2011. Creating the open Wordnet Bahasa. In *Proceedings of the 25th Pacific Asia Conference on Language, Information and Computation (PACLIC 25)*, pages 258–267, Singapore.

Stephan Oepen and Daniel Flickinger. 1998. Towards systematic grammar profiling: Test suite technology ten years after. 12(4):411–436.

Stephan Oepen, Erik Velldal, Jan Tore Lønning, Paul Meurer, Victoria Rosén, and Dan Flickinger. 2007. Towards hybrid quality-oriented machine translation: On linguistics and probabilities in MT. In *Proceedings of the 10th International Conference on Theoretical and Methodological Issues in Machine Translation*, pages 144–153, Skövde, Sweden.

Carl Pollard and Ivan A Sag. 1994. *Head-driven phrase structure grammar*. University of Chicago Press.

Fam Rashel, Andry Luthfi, Arawinda Dinakaramani, and Ruli Manurung. 2014. Building an Indonesian Rule-Based Part-of-Speech Tagger. Kuching.

Yu Jie Seah and Francis Bond. 2014. Annotation of Pronouns in a Multilingual Corpus of Mandarin Chinese, English and Japanese.

Melanie Siegel and Emily M. Bender. 2002. Efficient Deep Processing of Japanese. In *Proceedings of the 3rd Workshop on Asian Language Resources and International Standardization at the 19th International Conference on Computational Linguistics*, Taipei.

James Neil Sneddon, Alexander Adelaar, Dwi Noverini Djenar, and Michael C. Ewing. 2010. *Indonesian Reference Grammar*. Allen & Unwin, New South Wales, 2 edition.

Sebastian Sulger, Miriam Butt, Tracy Holloway King, Paul Meurer, Tibor Laczkó, György Rákosi, Cheikh M Bamba Dione, Helge Dyvik, Victoria Rosén, Koenraad De Smedt, et al. 2013. Pargrambank: The pargram parallel treebank. In *ACL (1)*, pages 550–560.

Liling Tan and Francis Bond. 2012. Building and annotating the linguistically diverse NTU-MC (NTU-multilingual corpus). 22(4):161–174.

An HPSG-based Shared-Grammar for the Chinese Languages: ZHONG [|]

Zhenzhen Fan◇♠ **Sanghoun Song**♠ **Francis Bond**♠
◇Institute of Systems Science, National University of Singapore
♠Division of Linguistics and Multilingual Studies, Nanyang Technological University
Singapore
zhenzhen@nus.edu.sg, {sanghoun,fcbond}@ntu.edu.sg

Abstract

This paper introduces our attempts to model the Chinese language using HPSG and MRS. Chinese refers to a family of various languages including Mandarin Chinese, Cantonese, Min, etc. These languages share a large amount of structure, though they may differ in orthography, lexicon, and syntax. To model these, we are building a family of grammars: ZHONG [|]. This grammar contains instantiations of various Chinese languages, sharing descriptions where possible. Currently we have prototype grammars for Cantonese and Mandarin in both simplified and traditional script, all based on a common core. The grammars also have facilities for robust parsing, sentence generation, and unknown word handling.

1 Introduction

Chinese is a group of related but sometimes mutually unintelligible languages that originated in China, including Mandarin Chinese, Cantonese, Min, etc. These languages have many grammatical similarities, though their orthography, vocabulary and syntax all differ from language to language. Thus, it is advantageous to implement a Chinese resource capable of covering both the common parts of the grammars and the linguistic diversity across the languages. Building an integrated grammar reduces the cost for resource construction and also helps the system reflect the genuine nature of the Chinese languages reliably.

This paper reports on our on-going project of building up an integrated computational grammar for these languages (ZHONG [|]) within the HPSG and MRS frameworks (Pollard and Sag, 1994; Copestake et al., 2005). The grammar is implemented using the collection of language processing tools offered by the DELPH-IN (DEep Linguistic Processing with HPSG - INitiative, `http://www.delph-in.net`) consortium. This grammar combines a shared core for all the Chinese languages, as well as language specific descriptions. Currently we only have grammars for Mandarin Chinese (with simplified and traditional characters) and Cantonese, although we hope to add Min soon.

This paper describes how the grammar has been constructed and reports on its current capacity for parsing and generation. The paper is structured as follows: Section 2 offers background knowledge of the current work. Section 3 presents how the resource grammar works for the different Chinese languages. After discussing the specification of the grammar in Section 4, Section 5 conducts an evaluation to see coverage. Section 6 concludes this paper with an outlook for future work.

2 Background

2.1 Frameworks

The grammatical framework used for creating the Chinese shared-grammar is Head-driven Phrase Structure Grammar. HPSG models human language in a monostratal way via unification of constraints. Rules in HPSG are constructed as feature structures, which allows constructions to be analyzed via multiple inheritance hierarchies modelling the fact that constructions cluster into groups with a family resemblance that corresponds to a constraint on a common supertype.

The meaning representation system our grammar employs is Minimal Recursion Semantics. MRS representations have two significant characteristics. First, MRS introduces a flat representation expressing meanings by feature structures. Second, MRS takes advantage of underspecification for handling quantifier scopes and others, which allows flexibility in representation.

Proceedings of the Grammar Engineering Across Frameworks (GEAF) Workshop, 53rd Annual Meeting of the ACL and 7th IJCNLP, pages 17–24,
Beijing, China, July 26-31, 2015. ©2015 Association for Computational Linguistics

2.2 DELPH-IN

DELPH-IN is an informal collaboration between linguists and computer scientists adopting HPSG and MRS. DELPH-IN employs a shared format for grammatical representation based on type feature structures. The repository DELPH-IN readily provides consists of open-source tools, computational grammars, and language resources.

The tools include grammar development environment (LKB (Copestake, 2002)), efficient parsers/generators for language processing (PET (Callmeier, 2000), ACE (`http://sweaglesw.org/linguistics/ace`), *agree* (Slayden, 2012)), dynamic treebanking tools ([incr tsdb()] (Oepen, 2001), ACE), machine translation engine (LOGON, ACE, *agree*), and stochastic models to select the most plausible interpretation. The collection of DELPH-IN grammars described in Type Definition Language include ERG for English (Flickinger, 2000), Jacy for Japanese (Siegel and Bender, 2002), GG for German (Crysmann, 2003), SRG for Spanish (Marimon, 2012), KRG for Korean (Kim et al., 2011), and others. The language resources contain test sets parsed with DELPH-IN grammars, such as the Redwoods Treebank in English (Oepen et al., 2004) and the Hinoki Treebank in Japanese (Bond et al., 2006), and a set of transfer rules (e.g. JaEn, (Bond et al., 2011)).

2.3 Previous Work on Chinese HPSG

2.3.1 Early Work

Early work on Chinese HPSG can be traced back to the 1990s, typically focusing on pure linguistic analysis of specific phenomena in Mandarin Chinese, such as the Chinese reflexive *ziji* (Xue et al., 1994), complement structure (Xue and McFetridge, 1996), and Chinese NPs (Gao, 1994; Xue and McFetridge, 1995; Ng, 1997).

Efforts towards a more comprehensive analysis of Mandarin Chinese in the framework of HPSG are documented in two PhD theses. The analysis in Gao (2000) covers topic sentences, valence alternations (including BA, ZAI, and other constructions), hierarchical argument structures, locative phrases, phrase structures, and resultative structures. The work of Li (2001) focuses more on the definition of word in Chinese for the problem of ambiguity in word segmentation, as well as two borderline problems between compounding/morphology and syntax - separable verbs and Chinese derivation and affixes.

2.3.2 Computational Grammars

In more recent work, in-depth analysis continues to be conducted on specific phenomena in Chinese HPSG, like the detailed account of Serial Verb Constructions (SVC) (Müller and Lipenkova, 2009), reanalysis of BA structure (Lipenkova, 2011), valence alternations and marking structures (Lipenkova, 2013), etc. However, the trend is to extend pure linguistic analysis to implementation of the grammar as a more general computational resource. This has led to a few independently developed HPSG grammars on Mandarin Chinese with MRS as the semantic representation format: ManGO (Yang, 2007), MCG (Zhang et al., 2011), and ChinGram (Müller and Lipenkova, 2013). ChinGram was implemented in the grammar development system TRALE (Meurers et al., 2002), whereas ManGO and MCG were developed using LKB and the LinGO Grammar Matrix customization system (Bender et al., 2010). These grammars cover a wide variety of core linguistic phenomena in Mandarin Chinese, but have limited lexical coverage as they typically only provide lexical entries for the words appearing in focused testsuites. Yu et al. (2010), on the other hand, has explored a semi-automatic approach to developing a Chinese HPSG parser by proposing a skeleton design of the grammar and then learning a lexicon from an HPSG Treebank manually converted from the Penn Chinese Treebank 6.0 (Xue et al., 2005).

The foundation of our work is ManGO. Its testsuite is a Mandarin Chinese version of the MRS testsuite used by the ERG, with short example sentences covering a wide range of phenomena such as intransitive, transitive, and ditransitive verbs, BA and BEI structures, clausal subjects/objects, aspect markers, prepositional and adverbial adjuncts, possessives, classifiers, numerals and determiners for noun phrases, predicative and attributive adjectives, locative and temporal phrases, nominalization, questions, imperative clauses, coordinations, etc. Its lexicon contains 231 lexical entries for 192 unique terms in 76 lexical types.

3 ZHONG [|]

The idea of letting different grammars share a common core to capture cross-linguistic generalization has been embraced by a number of projects as a more systematic approach for grammar development. The LinGO Grammar Matrix system (Bender et al., 2010) expedites the development of complex grammars through grammar customization by providing a static core grammar that handles basic phrase types, semantic compositionality and general infrastructure. It also provides libraries for cross-linguistically variable phenomena, so that analyses of these can be dynamically generated as code based on user-configured parameters. The generated grammar is then extended usually manually by a grammar engineer. CoreGram (Müller, 2013) is motivated by a similar assumption that grammars sharing certain properties can be grouped into classes and thus share common files. Fokkens et al. (2012) proposes CLIMB (Comparative Libraries of Implementations with Matrix Basis), a methodology closely related to the LinGO Grammar Matrix. While still sharing implementation across different languages, the emphasis of CLIMB is facilitating the exploration and comparison of implementations of different analyses for the same phenomenon.

There's also existing work sharing a common core grammar among languages within a language family. Avgustinova and Zhang (2009) builds a common Slavic core grammar (SlaviCore) shared by a closed set of languages in the Slavic language family. They further extended their work into SlaviCLIMB (Fokkens and Avgustinova, 2013), a dynamic grammar engineering component based on the CLIMB methodology, to capture language specific variations and facilitate grammar development for individual Slavic languages.

Extending the grammar development beyond Mandarin Chinese, ZHONG [|] aims to provide a shared-grammar for Chinese and model various varieties of Chinese in a single hierarchy. The different Chinese grammars share some elements, such as basic word order, and separate other elements, such as lexemes and specific grammar rules (e.g., classifier constructions).

All grammars inherit from three common cores, viz. `zhong.tdl`, `zhong-lextypyes.tdl`, and `zhong-letypes.tdl`. Building upon the common constraints. Mandarin and Cantonese inherit from `cmn.tdl` and `yue.tdl`, respectively. The distinctions between Mandarin and Cantonese captured so far include the expression of definiteness, classifiers, sentence final particles, aspect hierarchy, and some vocabulary. The Mandarin Chinese grammars are further divided into `zhs` and `zht` depending on whether the set of strings consists of simplified characters or traditional characters. These two further inherit from `zhs.tdl` and `zht.tdl`, respectively. The official webpage of ZHONG [|], with demo and test results, is `http://moin.delph-in.net/ZhongTop`, and the entire data set can be freely downloaded from `https://github.com/delph-in/zhong`.

The size of the current grammar is presented in Table 1. ManGO, which ZHONG [|] stems from, was created using the LinGO Grammar Matrix customization system. Hence, there are many fundamental types shared with the Grammar Matrix's core (`matrix.tdl`).

Table 1: Size of grammar

items	common	cmn	zhs	zht	yue
types	383	21	1,017	7	17
phrase rules	79	0	0	0	0
lexical rules	69	4	3	0	2
lex-entry types	89	5	0	0	9
lexicon	–	–	43,067	17,470	903
testsuites	–	–	16	1	3

4 Components

4.1 Preprocessing and Postprocessing

ZHONG [|] includes an unknown word handling module based on the chart-mapping technique of Adolphs et al. (2008). We have built a pipeline for converting raw text into a segmented POS-based lattice for input to the parser. The preprocessing stage for handling unknown words runs with the Stanford tools including the Chinese word segmenter (Tseng et al., 2005) and the Chinese Part-Of-Speech tagger (Toutanova et al., 2003). There are multiple different standards for segmenting the input string in Chinese, viz. Chinese Penn Treebank and Peking University. Between them, we are using the former because our fundamental development corpus NTU-MC (Tan and Bond, 2012) was segmented using that standard. We implemented a wrapper to run these tools in the pipeline using NLTK (Bird, 2006). In addition, the pre-processor includes some generic lexical entry rules for handling particular string patterns, such as numbers, dates, currency, emails, urls, etc. These lattice-based mapping rules work with a set of regular expressions. Building upon these two facilities, many lexical items not registered in the dictionary can be automatically identified and efficiently processed.

For postprocessing, we implemented a monolingual transfer grammar for paraphrasing simplified Mandarin Chinese, viz. `ZsZs`. This converts

MRS outputs in the parse results into more generic or more specific ones. Currently, this postprocessor works for generating intensifying constructions and classifier constructions.

4.2 Lexical Acquisition

As ManGO's lexicon was small, our first task was to expand the lexical coverage of Zhong quickly. Our approach is to semi-automatically learn lexical entries from annotated corpora, starting from the sample of Sinica Treebank (**sinica**, Huang et al. (2000)) distributed with NLTK package and the Penn Chinese Treebank (**pctb**, Xue et al. (2005)) for Mandarin Chinese. Our main source at the beginning was **sinica** as it has a comprehensive set of POS tags, especially for verb subcategorization. Its POS tags were manually mapped to Zhong's lexical types after careful study. Lexical entries for the mapped types were then created automatically. The tags from **pctb** are more coarse. We acquire words for the lexical types we are interested in by matching specific tree patterns against the treebank. The work is still ongoing.

As Zhong is used for both parsing and generation, we also try to learn additional information for the lexical entries, which is often required to constrain the grammar from generating unwanted sentences. For example, a list of classifiers (CL) can be readily learned from **sinica** and **pctb**. However, since in Mandarin Chinese there is a selective association between the sortal classifiers and the nouns, this association needs to be modeled so that during generation, a correct classifier can be selected for a certain noun. Our solution is to automatically build a frequency-based dictionary of noun-CL pairs, by extracting frequency information from a very large corpus. The corpus we used includes the latest dump of the Chinese Wikipedia, the second version of Chinese Gigaword (Graff et al., 2005), and the UM-Corpus (Tian et al., 2014). This data was cleaned, sentence delimited and converted to simplified Chinese script. It was further preprocessed using the Stanford Segmentor and POS tagger. Using very restrictive POS patterns, CL-noun pairs are extracted and filtered against a list of 204 sortal-CLs provided by Huang (Huang et al., 1997). They are then added into a lemma-based dictionary together with their frequency information. This lemma-based dictionary is further expanded into concept-based dictionary by mapping the lemmas to the concepts in the Chinese Open Wordnet (Wang and Bond, 2013). The frequency information and possible CLs for matched senses are propagated to upper level through the union of CLs and respective sum of frequencies. Generation test on a set of held-out data reports a human validated performance of 88% on generation of classifiers using the concept-based dictionary and 80% using the lemma-based dictionary, whereas a baseline approach, taking 个 *ge* as the CL for every entry, gives 44.7%.

4.3 Configuration

ZHONG [|] has been built up following the premise "parsing robustly and generating strictly" (Bond et al., 2008). This means that even a rather infelicitous sentence should be parsed, but the infelicitous sentence should be filtered out in generation. This different approach to parsing and generation can be facilitated using different configurations for compiling grammars. First, ZHONG [|] includes a flag feature [STYLE *style*] for marking the felicity of particular lexical items and constructions, whose subtypes are *strict*, *robust*, *unproductive*, etc. Second, there are different types of roots: namely, `roots.tdl`, `roots-robust.tdl`, and `roots-strict.tdl`. The first one works for ordinary parsing and generation, the second one works with bridging rules to fill out the chasm between constructions, and the third one is particularly used for generation with the [STYLE *strict*] flag. Third, there are different scripts to load and compile the grammars within LKB and ACE, such as `config.tdl`, `config-robust.tdl`, and `config-strict.tdl`. The last one includes the list of items and rules that should be ignored in generation (`generation.ignore`).

For example, 去着 'go DUR' may not sound good to Chinese native speakers, because the verb 去 tends not to co-occur with the durative aspect. Our grammar provides a parse tree for the sentence with a flag [STYLE *robust*] but does not generate such a sentence. To take another example, the punctuation markers are optionally treated in the ordinary and robust processing but obligatorily appear in the generation output produced by the grammar compiled by `config-strict.tdl`.

4.4 Grammar Enhancement

We have been enhancing the grammar with the objective to achieve coherent and consistent semantics constrained by syntax. Using the sentences

Table 2: Grammar enhancement

	what we improved	what we added	what we plan to do
grammar	topic-comment clefts BA and BEI NP structures classifiers argument structure adpositions	reduplication VV compounds A-not-A questions particles fragments interjections honorification	relative clauses nominalization serial verbs conjunctions
engineering	generation	unknown word handling bridging rules test modules full-forest treebanking	Wordnet incorporation transfer rules machine translation

from the MRS testsuite, and supplemented by sentences collected from relevant literature and real corpus, we have improved the grammar on its handling of the known structures in the MRS testsuite, such as BA and BEI structures, NP structures, argument structures, classifiers, etc. At the same time, we have also created analyses to cover linguistically interesting phenomena new to the MRS testsuite, including reduplication of adjectives, resultative VV compounds, A-not-A questions, as well as the handling of particles, interjections, and fragments. Our work is summarized in Table 2.[1]

4.5 Full-forest Treebanking

Using the simplified Mandarin Chinese grammar constructed thus far, we annotated two data sets by means of the full-forest treebanking tool (Packard, 2015). The data sets include the MRS Matrix testsuite in simplified Mandarin Chinese (`http://moin.delph-in.net/MatrixMrsTestSuite`) and the first 101 sentences in a novel (斑点带子案, *The Adventure of the Speckled Band* written by Arthur Conan Doyle, translated into Mandarin Chinese). The first set is a standard testsuite used in DELPH-In for testing grammars' coverage of simple semantic phenomena. Of the 107 sentences, 102 can be parsed with the current grammar. Of these, 14 outputs were rejected in the annotation because no parse tree licenses the desired semantics. The second test suite was chosen because there exists a comparable annotated corpus written in four other languages (English, Spanish, Russian, and Korean) (Song, 2014). Because this is a running text consisting of longer sentences, the parse coverage is still poor: 12 out of 101. Of these 12, 8 were rejected for inadequate semantics. Annotating this running text, we learned that the current grammar does not properly process relative clauses and serial verb constructions. These two phenomena are at the top of our agenda for grammar improvement.

[1]The implementation of each grammatical phenomenon provided in Table 2 will be separately discussed in a series of upcoming papers.

5 Evaluation

We measured the coverage of the current grammar focusing on simplified Mandarin Chinese (abbreviated to `zhs`). We have two groups of test suites. First, we use three linguistic phenomena-based testsuites: the testsuite constructed at Free University of Berlin (**fu-berlin**, Müller and Lipenkova (2013)), the testsuite of the Mandarin Chinese Grammar (**mcg-wxl**, Zhang et al. (2011)), and the JEC basic sentences (**jec**, Kawahara and Kurohashi (2006)). Second, we use naturally occurring texts in order to check the computational feasibility of the current implementation. The corpora we used include the NTU-MC (**ntumc**, Tan and Bond (2012)), the Penn Chinese Treebank (**pctb**, Xue et al. (2005)), and the Sinica Treebank (**sinica**, Huang et al. (2000)). We used the entire NTU-MC (7,460 sentences) and extracted the first 5,000 sentences from the other two corpora. The tools for running tests are pyDelphin (`https://github.com/goodmami/pydelphin`) and gTest (`https://github.com/goodmami/gtest`). The result of coverage testing is provided in Table 3.

The numbers in parenthesis stand for the coverage of ungrammatical sentences. Note that only the first two include ungrammatical items. Since ungrammatical sentences had better be rejected, the smaller number means the better performance for those items. All the numbers in parenthesis are smaller than 5%, which shows that our grammar does not overgenerate very much.

When unknown word handling (**unk**) is facilitated, our current grammar provides relatively satisfactory results, as indicated in the third column.

Table 3: Coverage of simplified Mandarin (%)

testsuite	plain	unk	br	unk+br	gen	end-to-end-success
fu-berlin	22.22 (3.11)	80.25 (3.12)	22.22 (4.89)	97.53 (4.97)	90.91	20.20
mcg-wxl	57.28 (3.80)	66.3 (3.78)	82.44 (5.00)	99.37 (5.00)	92.94	53.24
jec	13.33	41.16	27.04	79.34	90.10	12.01
ntumc	3.47	15.58	10.54	47.82	70.54	2.45
pctb	0.84	7.10	10.18	43.70	42.86	0.36
sinica	3.88	40.36	6.52	65.00	80.41	3.12

However, the parsing coverage is still low when a running text is chosen for testing. Particularly, when it comes to the **pctb** testsuite, the coverage is only about 7%. There are two main reasons. First, the sentences in the **pctb** testsuite are much longer than those in the other testsuites. Second, our current grammar has not fully modeled relative clauses and serial verbs in Chinese, but the **pctb** testsuite includes many sentences containing such constructions. Thus, our immediate goal in grammar construction is to implement the constructions (see Table 2). When the **sinica** testsuite is used, the coverage is relatively high (40.36%). This is mainly because our lexical acquisition is mostly based on the corpus.

Using bridging rules (**br**) aims to facilitate robust parsing, which serves to minimize additional parsing costs (time and space) and maximize compatibility with existing platforms and tools. Since a set of bridging rules allows any two signs to combine into a phrase, the combination of unknown word handling and bridging rules (**unk+br**) provides the highest coverage, as indicated in the fifth column of Table 3. This implies that the **unk+br** mode enables our grammar to be used for training of statistical models and run-time applications in future work.

The generation coverage (**gen**) is calculated as follows: If a sentence is parsed, the MRS representation of the parse result is chosen as the input source for generation. Because the generation does not work with unknown word handling within the present infrastructure, the input source comes from the parse result of **plain**. If the generation process successfully produces one or more surface forms at the end, the generation coverage grows up. Notice that the generation coverage is not necessarily 100%, because the memory space for generation is limited (2GB in the current evaluation). The held-out testsuites result in more than 90% generation coverage, and the testsuites consisting of naturally occurring texts result in more than 70% except the **pctb** testsuite. We believe that these measures are good for such a young grammar, although several challenging points remain. Finally, the end-to-end-success coverage from parsing to generation is measured by multiplying the values in the second column (**plain**) and the sixth column (**gen**).

6 Outlook

We will continue to enhance ZHONG [|] to handle the linguistic phenomena needed to parse our corpora (particularly, NTU-MC). Some of the tasks on the immediate agenda are: relative clauses, variations of nominalization, serial verb construction, conjunctions, other forms of verbal compounds, and more reduplication patterns. Lexical acquisition for `zht` and `yue` will also be performed to expand their lexical coverage.

We will also treebank other corpora, both as feedback to the grammarians and as a source of information on the distribution of phenomena (essential to training parse ranking models). As coverage increases we will exploit ZHONG [|] and other DELPH-IN grammars to build machine translation systems to and from Chinese.

Acknowledgments

We would like to express special thanks to Justin Chunlei Yang and Dan Flickinger for their enormous work on ManGO, which our current grammar is based on. In addition, we received much inspiration from Yi Zhang and Rui Wang and their Mandarin Chinese Grammar. We are grateful to Michael Wayne Goodman, Luis Mortado da Costa, Bo Chen, Joanna Sio Ut Seong, Shan Wang, František Kratochvíl, Huizhen Wang, Wenjie Wang, Giulia Bonansinga, David Moeljadi, Tuấn Anh Lê, Woodley Packard, Leslie Lee, and Jong-Bok Kim for their help and comments. Valuable comments from four anonymous reviewers are also much appreciated. Of course, we are solely responsible for all the remaining errors and infelicities. This research was supported in part by the MOE Tier 2 grant *That's what you meant: a Rich Representation for Manipulation of Meaning* (MOE ARC41/13).

References

Peter Adolphs, Stephan Oepen, Ulrich Callmeier, Berthold Crysmann, Dan Flickinger, and Bernd Kiefer. 2008. Some Fine Points of Hybrid Natural Language Parsing. In Nicoletta Calzolari (Conference Chair), Khalid Choukri, Bente Maegaard, Joseph Mariani, Jan Odijk, Stelios Piperidis, and Daniel Tapias, editors, *Proceedings of the Sixth International Language Resources and Evaluation*, pages 1380–1387, Marrakech, Morocco.

Tania Avgustinova and Yi Zhang. 2009. Parallel Grammar Engineering for Slavic Languages. In *Workshop on Grammar Engineering Across Frameworks at the ACL/IJCNLP*.

Emily M. Bender, Scott Drellishak, Antske Fokkens, Laurie Poulson, and Safiyyah Saleem. 2010. Grammar Customization. *Research on Language & Computation*, 8(1):23–72.

Steven Bird. 2006. NLTK: the Natural Language Toolkit. In *Proceedings of the COLING/ACL on Interactive presentation sessions*, pages 69–72.

Francis Bond, Sanae Fujita, and Takaaki Tanaka. 2006. The Hinoki Syntactic and Semantic Treebank of Japanese. *Language Resources and Evaluation*, 40(3–4):253–261.

Francis Bond, Eric Nichols, Darren Scott Appling, and Michael Paul. 2008. Improving Statistical Machine Translation by Paraphrasing the Training Data. In *Proceedings of the International Workshop on Spoken Language Translation*, pages 150–157, Hawaii.

Francis Bond, Stephan Oepen, Eric Nichols, Dan Flickinger, Erik Velldal, and Petter Haugereid. 2011. Deep Open-Source Machine Translation. *Machine Translation*, 25(2):87–105.

Ulrich Callmeier. 2000. PET – a Platform for Experimentation with Efficient HPSG Processing Techniques. *Natural Language Engineering*, 6(1):99–107.

Ann Copestake, Dan Flickinger, Carl Pollard, and Ivan A. Sag. 2005. Minimal Recursion Semantics: An Introduction. *Research on Language & Computation*, 3(4):281–332.

Ann Copestake. 2002. *Implementing Typed Feature Structure Grammars*. CSLI Publications, Stanford, CA.

Berthold Crysmann. 2003. On the Efficient Implementation of German Verb Placement in HPSG. In *Proceedings of RANLP 2003*, pages 112–116, Borovets, Bulgaria.

Dan Flickinger. 2000. On Building a More Efficient Grammar by Exploiting Types. *Natural Language Engineering*, 6(1):15–28.

Antske Fokkens and Tania Avgustinova. 2013. SlaviCLIMB: Combining Expertise for Slavic Grammar Development using a Metagrammar. In *Workshop on High-level Methodologies for Grammar Engineering*, pages 87–92.

Antske Fokkens, Tania Avgustinova, and Yi Zhang. 2012. CLIMB Grammars: Three Projects using Metagrammar Engineering. In *Proceedings of the Eight International Conference on Language Resources and Evaluation*, pages 1672–1679, Istanbul.

Qian Gao. 1994. Chinese NP Structure. *Linguistics*, 32:475–510.

Qian Gao. 2000. *Argument Structure, HPSG, and Chinese grammar*. Ph.D. thesis, Ohio State University.

David Graff, Ke Chen, Junbo Kong, and Kazuaki Maeda. 2005. *Chinese Gigaword Second Edition LDC2005T14*. Web Download. Linguistic Data Consortium.

Chu-Ren Huang, Keh-Jiann Chen, and Ching-Hsiung Lai, editors. 1997. *Mandarin Daily Dictionary of Chinese Classifiers*. Mandarin Daily Press, Taipei.

Chu-Ren Huang, Feng-Yi Chen, Keh-Jiann Chen, Zhao-ming Gao, and Kuang-Yu Chen. 2000. Sinica Treebank: Design Criteria, Annotation Guidelines, and On-line Interface. In *Proceedings of the Second Workshop on Chinese Language Processing*, pages 29–37, Hong Kong.

Daisuke Kawahara and Sadao Kurohashi. 2006. Case Frame Compilation from the Web using High-Performance Computing. In *Proceedings of the 5th International Conference on Language Resources and Evaluation*, pages 1344–1347, Genoa.

Jong-Bok Kim, Jaehyung Yang, Sanghoun Song, and Francis Bond. 2011. Deep Processing of Korean and the Development of the Korean Resource Grammar. *Linguistic Research*, 28(3):635–672.

Wei Li. 2001. *The Morpho-Syntactic Interface in a Chinese Phrase Structure*. Ph.D. thesis, Simon Fraser University.

Janna Lipenkova. 2011. Reanalysis of Obligatory Modifiers as Complements in the Chinese *ba*-Construction. In *Proceedings of the 18th International Head-driven Phrase Structure Grammar Conference, Stanford: CSLI Publications*.

Janna Lipenkova. 2013. Valence Alternations and Marking Structures in a HPSG Grammar for Mandarin Chinese. In *Sixth International Joint Conference on Natural Language Processing*, pages 27–35.

Montserrat Marimon. 2012. The Spanish DELPH-IN Grammar. *Language Resources and Evaluation*, 47(2):371–397.

W Detmar Meurers, Gerald Penn, and Frank Richter. 2002. A Web-Based Instructional Platform for Constraint-Based Grammar Formalisms and Parsing. In *Proceedings of the ACL-02 Workshop on Effective Tools and Methodologies for Teaching Natural Language Processing and Computational Linguistics-Volume 1*, pages 19–26.

Stefan Müller and Janna Lipenkova. 2009. Serial Verb Constructions in Chinese: An HPSG Account. In *Proceedings of the 16th International Conference on Head-Driven Phrase Structure Grammar*, pages 234–254.

Stefan Müller and Janna Lipenkova. 2013. ChinGram: A TRALE Implementation of an HPSG Fragment of Mandarin Chinese. In *Proceedings of the 27th Pacific Asia Conference on Language, Information, and Computation (PACLIC 27)*, pages 240–249, Taipei, Taiwan. Department of English, National Chengchi University.

Stefan Müller. 2013. The CoreGram Project: Theoretical Linguistics, Theory Development and Verification. *Ms. Freie Universität Berlin*.

Say Kiat Ng. 1997. A Double-Specifier Account of Chinese NPs Using Head-Driven Phrase Structure Grammar. MSc Thesis, Department of Linguistics, University of Edinburgh.

Stephan Oepen, Dan Flickinger, Kristina Toutanova, and Christoper D. Manning. 2004. LinGO Redwoods: A Rich and Dynamic Treebank for HPSG. *Research on Language & Computation*, 2(4):575–596.

Stephan Oepen. 2001. [incr tsdb()] — Competence and Performance Laboratory. User Manual. Technical report, Computational Linguistics, Saarland University.

Woodley Packard. 2015. Full Forest Treebanking. Master's thesis, University of Washington.

Carl Pollard and Ivan A. Sag. 1994. *Head-Driven Phrase Structure Grammar*. The University of Chicago Press, Chicago, IL.

Melanie Siegel and Emily M. Bender. 2002. Efficient Deep Processing of Japanese. In *Proceedings of the 3rd Workshop on Asian Language Resources and International Standardization*, pages 1–8, Taipei.

Glenn C. Slayden. 2012. Array TFS Storage for Unification Grammars. Master's thesis, University of Washington.

Sanghoun Song. 2014. *A Grammar Library for Information Structure*. Ph.D. thesis, University of Washington.

Liling Tan and Francis Bond. 2012. Building and Annotating the Linguistically Diverse NTU-MC (NTU-Multilingual Corpus). *International Journal of Asian Language Processing*, 22(4):161–174.

Liang Tian, Derek F. Wong, Lidia S. Chao, Paulo Quaresma, Francisco Oliveira, and Lu Yi. 2014. UM-Corpus: A Large English-Chinese Parallel Corpus for Statistical Machine Translation. In *Proceedings of the Ninth International Conference on Language Resources and Evaluation (LREC-2014)*. European Language Resources Association (ELRA).

Kristina Toutanova, Dan Klein, Christopher D Manning, and Yoram Singer. 2003. Feature-rich Part-of-Speech Tagging with a Cyclic Dependency Network. In *Proceedings of the 2003 Conference of the North American Chapter of the Association for Computational Linguistics on Human Language Technology-Volume 1*, pages 173–180.

Huihsin Tseng, Pichuan Chang, Galen Andrew, Daniel Jurafsky, and Christopher Manning. 2005. A Conditional Random Field Word Segmenter. In *Proceedings of the Fourth SIGHAN Workshop on Chinese Language Processing*, pages 169–171.

Shan Wang and Francis Bond. 2013. Building the Chinese Open Wordnet (COW): Starting from Core Synsets. In *Proceedings of the 11th Workshop on Asian Language Resources, a Workshop at IJCNLP-2013*, pages 10–18, Nagoya.

Ping Xue and Paul McFetridge. 1995. DP Structure, HPSG and the Chinese NP. In *Proceedings of the 14th Annual Conference of Canadian Linguistics Association*.

Ping Xue and Paul McFetridge. 1996. Complement Structure in Chinese. In *Proceedings of the 32nd Annual Meeting of the Chicago Lingusitic Society (CLS '96)*, Chicago, IL.

Ping Xue, Carl Pollard, and Ivan A Sag. 1994. A New Perspective on Chinese *ziji*. In *the Proceedings of the Thirteenth West Coast Conference on Formal Linguistics*.

Naiwen Xue, Fei Xia, Fu-Dong Chiou, and Marta Palmer. 2005. The Penn Chinese TreeBank: Phrase Structure Annotation of a Large Corpus. *Natural Language Engineering*, 11(02):207–238.

Chunlei Yang. 2007. *Expert Systems for Pragmatic Interpretations of ziji and Quantified Noun Phrases in HPSG*. Ph.D. thesis, Shanghai International Studies University.

Kun Yu, Yusuke Miyao, Xiangli Wang, Takuya Matsuzaki, and Junichi Tsujii. 2010. Semi-automatically Developing Chinese HPSG Grammar from the Penn Chinese Treebank for Deep Parsing. In *Proceedings of the 23rd International Conference on Computational Linguistics*, pages 1417–1425.

Yi Zhang, Rui Wang, and Yu Chen. 2011. Engineering a Deep HPSG for Mandarin Chinese. In *Proceedings of the 9th Workshop On Asian Language Resources*, Chiang Mai.

Parsing Chinese with a Generalized Categorial Grammar

Manjuan Duan **William Schuler**
Department of Linguistics
The Ohio State University
{duan,schuler}@ling.osu.edu

Abstract

Categorial grammars are attractive because they have a clear account of unbounded dependencies. This accounting is especially important in Mandarin Chinese which makes extensive usage of unbounded dependencies. However, parsers trained on existing categorial grammar annotations (Tse and Curran, 2010) extracted from the Penn Chinese Treebank (Xue et al., 2005) are not as accurate as those trained on the original treebank, possibly because enforcing a small set of inference rules in these grammars leads to large sets of categories, which cause sparse data problems. This work reannotates the Penn Chinese Treebank into a generalized categorial grammar which uses a larger rule set and a substantially smaller category set while retaining the capacity to model unbounded dependencies. Experimental results show a statistically significant improvement in parsing accuracy with this categorial grammar.

1 Introduction

Categorial grammar annotations are attractive because they have a transparent syntactic-semantic interface and provide a natural account of traces (Rimell et al., 2009; Nguyen et al., 2012). This is especially important in parsing Chinese, which generates 1.5 times as many traces as English and makes heavy use of unbounded dependencies (Kummerfeld et al., 2013). Unfortunately, the accuracy of parsers trained on existing categorial grammar reannotations (Chinese CCGbank; Tse and Curran, 2010) of the Penn Chinese Treebank (Xue et al., 2005) is much lower than that of parsers trained on the original Treebank (Tse and Curran, 2012). This may be because previous attempts used Combinatory Categorial Grammar (CCG; Steedman, 2000; Steedman, 2012), which is strongly lexicalized (Karttunen, 1989), using a small set of language-independent rules and consequently a large set of language-dependent categories. This strong lexicalization may contribute to sparse data problems.

This work reannotates the Penn Chinese Treebank into a 'moderately lexicalized' generalized categorial grammar, similar to that defined for English by Nguyen et al (2012), which uses a larger set of language-specific inference rules and a substantially smaller category set. Experimental results show a statistically significant gain in parsing accuracy from this moderately lexicalized grammar over parsing with a strongly lexicalized CCG.

2 Grammar Framework

A generalized categorial grammar (GCG; Bach, 1981; Nguyen et al., 2012)[1] is a tuple $\langle P, O, R, W, M \rangle$ (Oehrle, 1994) consisting of a set P of primitive category types, a set O of type-constructing operators, a set R of inference rules, a set W of vocabulary items, and a mapping M from vocabulary items to complex category types. A set of complex category types C may then be defined as: $P \subset C$; $C \times O \times C \subset C$; nothing else is in C.

The mapping M in a GCG defines a category type c and a constraint function g encoded by each lexeme $w \in W$, using the notation $w \mapsto c : g$. Encoded constraints are expressed using dependency functions,[2] labeled with dependency types or argument position numbers: $\mathbf{f}_0$, $\mathbf{f}_1$, $\mathbf{f}_2$, etc. For example, a constraint function g may consist of a single '0'-labeled dependency to a constant 'people':

[1] Nguyen et al (2012) notate the '//' and '\\' operators of Bach (1981) as **-g** and **-h**, mnemonic for 'gap' and 'heavy shift'.

[2] Dependencies shown here can be interpreted as a shorthand for distributed representations of sentence meanings compatible with cognitive computational neuroscientific models of episodic memory (Schuler and Wheeler, 2014).

Proceedings of the Grammar Engineering Across Frameworks (GEAF) Workshop, 53rd Annual Meeting of the ACL and 7th IJCNLP, pages 25–32,
Beijing, China, July 26-31, 2015. ©2015 Association for Computational Linguistics

$\lambda_x\, (\mathbf{f}_0\, x)$=people.

3 Chinese Syntax in GCG

Chinese is typically an SVO language, but it also has several SOV constructions, such as the focus constructions triggered by *lian* 'even,' or the *ba* construction, where the affected patient is moved to the preverbal position. Most adverbial modifiers are pre-verbal and most nominal modifiers, including relative clauses, are pre-nominal.

The set of primitive category types for Mandarin Chinese, P, $P \subset C$, contains the following primitive categories, generally labeled with the part of speech of the head of the category:

- **V**: verb-headed clause
- **N**: noun-headed phrase or clause
- **D**: *de*-clause
- **C**: cardinal number
- **Q**: quantificational phrase
- **A**: adjectival phrase or nominal modifier
- **R**: adverbial phrase or verbal modifier
- **B**: verbal complement of *ba*
- **E**: verbal complement of *bei*

The set of type-constructing operators O for Mandarin Chinese includes **-a** and **-b** operators for unsatisfied requirements of preceding or succeeding arguments, **-c** and **-d** operators for unsatisfied requirements of preceding or succeeding conjuncts, and a **-g** operator for unsatisfied requirements of gap categories.[3] A GCG category consists of a primitive category followed by one or more unsatisfied dependencies, each consisting of an operator followed by another category.

The set of inference rules R is described below.

3.1 Argument composition

The basic operation of most categorial grammars is argument composition. However, unlike most categorial grammars, the GCG described in this paper defines composition rules to explicitly encode dependencies between lexical items. Specifically, inference rules for argument composition are defined as follows, where $c \in C$, $p \in P$ and each $\varphi \in \{\textbf{-a}, \textbf{-b}\} \times C$:

$$c{:}g \;\; p\varphi_{1..n\text{-}1}\textbf{-a}c{:}h \Rightarrow p\varphi_{1..n\text{-}1}{:}\lambda_x\, g\,(\mathbf{f}_n\, x) \wedge (h\, x) \quad \text{(Aa)}$$

$$p\varphi_{1..n\text{-}1}\textbf{-b}c{:}g \;\; c{:}h \Rightarrow p\varphi_{1..n\text{-}1}{:}\lambda_x\, (g\, x) \wedge h\,(\mathbf{f}_n\, x) \quad \text{(Ab)}$$

[3]Following (Nguyen et al., 2012), directional operators such as forward and backward slashes ('\' and '/') are not used because some operators, such as gap operators in tough constructions, are undirected.

The first composition rule Aa stipulates that when a predicate h of category $p\varphi_{1..n\text{-}1}\textbf{-a}c$ takes a preceding argument g of category c as its n-th argument, the syntactic dependency that g is h's n-th argument is added. The second composition rule Ab is an argument composition rule taking a succeeding argument.

3.2 Modifier composition

Inference rules for modifier composition apply preceding or succeeding modifiers of category p-$\mathbf{b}d$ to modificands of category c, where $p \in \{\mathbf{A}, \mathbf{R}\}$, $d \in \{\mathbf{N}, \mathbf{V}\}$:

$$p\text{-}\mathbf{b}d{:}g \;\; c{:}h \Rightarrow c{:}\lambda_x\, \exists_y\, (g\, y) \wedge (h\, x) \wedge (\mathbf{f}_1\, y){=}x \quad \text{(Ma)}$$

$$c{:}g \;\; p\text{-}\mathbf{b}d{:}h \Rightarrow c{:}\lambda_x\, \exists_y\, (g\, x) \wedge (h\, y) \wedge (\mathbf{f}_1\, y){=}x \quad \text{(Mb)}$$

The modifier composition rules Ma and Mb establish a '1'-labeled dependency from the modifier to the modificand. With argument and modifier composition rules, we can derive the Chinese sentence shown in (1).

(1) 'Shanghai, in the aspect of finance, develops fast.'

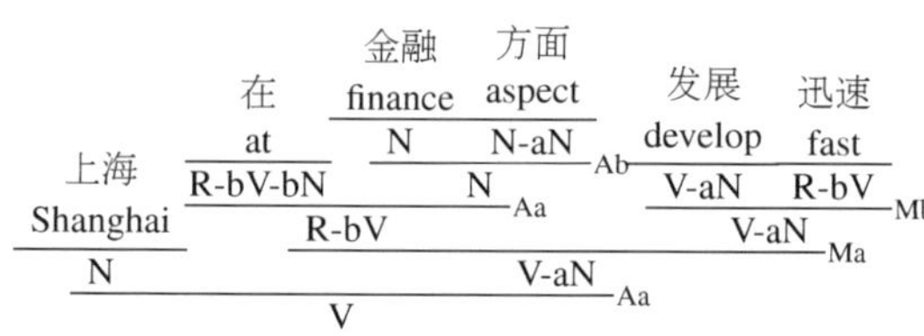

The separate modifier composition rules in GCG make it possible to reuse modifier categories across different contexts. For example, in (1), 在金融方面 'in the aspect of finance' is an adverbial modifier, having the category **R-bV**. It has the same category when the phrase is a sentential modifier as shown in (2). Consequently, 在 'at' in both (1) and (2) has the same category **R-bV-bN**, which means it takes a succeeding nominal argument to become an adverbial modifier.

(2) 'In the aspect of finance, Shanghai develops fast.'

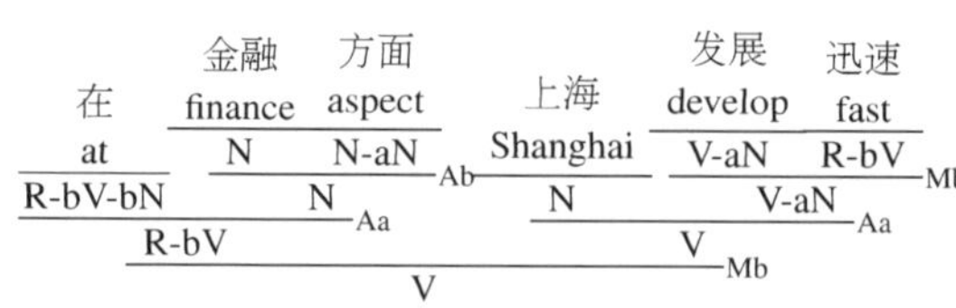

In contrast, since CCG enforces a restricted set of inference rules, it needs to provide two different categories, (S\NP)/(S\NP)/NP and S/S/NP for 在 in (1) and (2). In total, Chinese CCGbank has 91 different categories for 在, since the prepositional phrase headed by 在 can modify constituents of various syntactic categories. In contrast, Chinese GCG annotations only have 9 different categories for 在.

Another example of differing lexicalization is the category of the tense aspect 了 in Chinese, which can either occur immediately after a verb or after the whole verb phrase to indicate past tense. Although generalized backward crossed composition (Steedman, 2000) helps aspect/tense particles in Chinese usually retain their canonical category (S\NP)\(S\NP), there are still 59 different categories for 了 in Chinese CCGbank (Tse and Curran, 2010), and most of them are semantically indistinguishable.

3.3 Nominal and quantificational expressions

Mandarin Chinese does not have determiners such as 'the' or 'a' in English, so there is no empirical motivation to distinguish NP and N categories. However, *classifiers* or *measure words*, glossed as 'M' in (3), are obligatory when a noun is quantified by a number. This unit of measure is needed for quantification of nouns because the lack of number morphology in Chinese makes all nouns behave as mass nouns (Allan, 1977; Borer, 2005).

(3) 'three people'

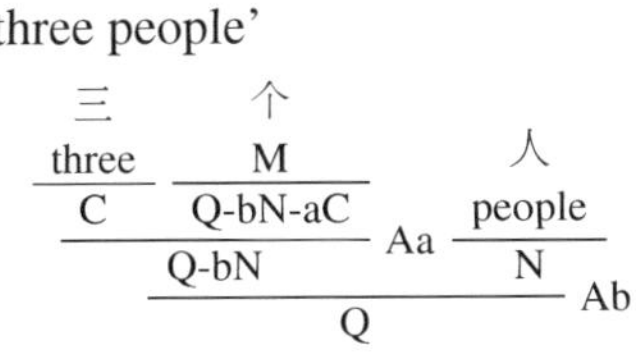

We propose a separate category Q for quantificational expressions because they can be predicative, as in (4), which makes them different from common nouns. A zero-head rule Z, where $c, d, e \in C$, converts the Q category to V-aN to make the quantificational expression predicative.

$$e{:}g \Rightarrow c\text{-}\mathbf{a}d{:}\lambda_x\,(\mathbf{f}_0\,x){=}\mathsf{pred} \wedge g\,(\mathbf{f}_2\,x) \qquad \text{(Z)}$$

(4) 'He is three.'

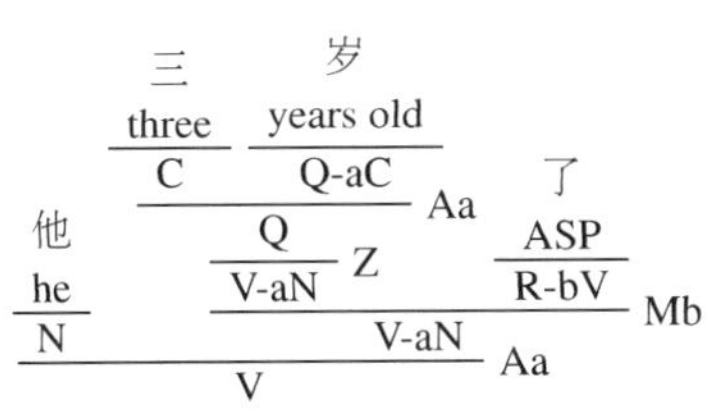

Classifiers like 年 'years,' 岁 'years-old' and 天 'day' already contain the nominal information, so they do not require nominal arguments like other classifiers. Classifiers of this type have a different category 'Q-aC' to reflect this combinational difference. By doing so, the numbers receive the same category C in both 三天 'three days,' and 三个人 'three people.' However, in both Chinese Treebank and CCGbank, the category 'M' is used for both types of classifiers, which results in numbers like 三 'three' having the category QP/M in 'three days' and the category (NP/NP)/M in 'three people' in Chinese CCGbank. This is not desirable because it expends training examples on an artificial distinction between the numbers 三 'three' in each of these expressions, which are semantically the same.

3.4 Topicalization

Topicalization in Mandarin can involve either movement of a topicalized constituent or not. The topicalization which involves movement is similar to that of English, in which the object is usually moved to the sentence initial position and a gap is left behind, as shown in (5).[4]

(5) 'The rice, I ate.'

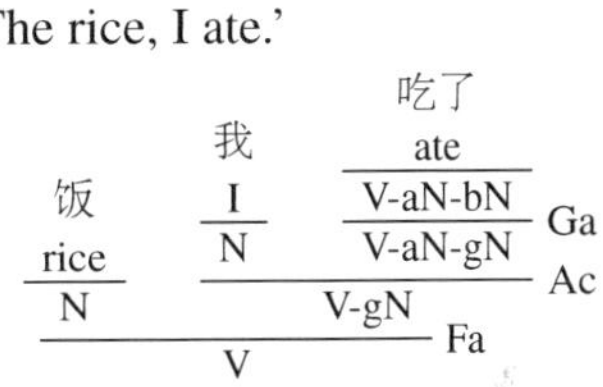

The non-movement topicalization occurs much more frequently in Mandarin, in which the subject of the sentence usually has an 'association' relation to the topic, as shown in (6).

(6) 'Of him, the appetite is good.'

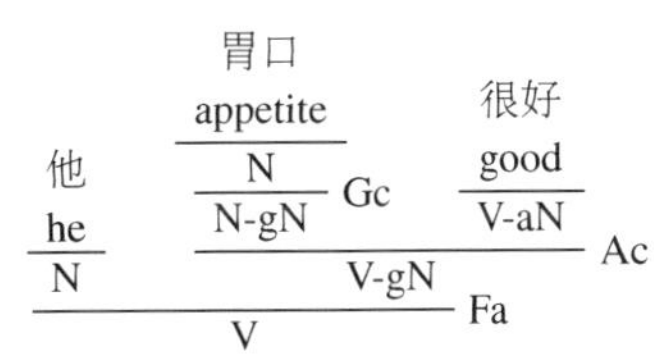

The referent of the subject in the non-movement topicalization needs to be further specified by the topic. Although topics are seen to be associated with other constituents of the sentence, especially in colloquial expressions, only associations with subjects are observed in the Treebank data. Therefore in our analysis of this type of topicalization, the subject undergoes a unary type conversion from N to N-gN to introduce a gap, which is

[4]The verb 吃 and the tense particle 了 are separate tokens, shown together here to simplify the derivation. We apply the same simplification to 很好 in following examples.

later discharged by the topic to capture the 'association' relation between the subject and the topic.

Inference rules for gap composition are:

$$p\varphi_{1..n\text{-}1}oc \Rightarrow p\varphi_{1..n\text{-}1}\textbf{-g}c{:}\lambda_{vx}(g\,x) \wedge (\mathbf{f}_n\,x){=}v \quad \text{(Ga)}$$

$$c{:}g \Rightarrow c\textbf{-g}d{:}\lambda_{vx}(g\,x) \wedge (\mathbf{f}_1\,v){=}x \quad \text{(Gb)}$$

$$\text{N}{:}g \Rightarrow \text{N}\textbf{-g}\text{N}{:}\lambda_{vx}(g\,x) \wedge \exists_e(\textbf{de-asso}\,e\,x\,v) \quad \text{(Gc)}$$

where $p \in P$, $o \in \{\textbf{-a}, \textbf{-b}\}$, $c \in C$, $d \in \{\textbf{A-bN}, \textbf{R-bV}\}$ and $\varphi \in \{\textbf{-a}, \textbf{-b}\} \times C$. Rule Ga hypothesizes a gap as a preceding or succeeding argument, rule Gb hypothesizes a nominal or adverbial modifier gap and rule Gc hypothesizes a gap which is associated with the subject in topicalization.

Non-local arguments, each consisting of a non-local operator and argument category $\psi \in \{\textbf{-g}\} \times C$, are then propagated to consequents from all possible combinations of antecedents. For $d{:}g\;\; e{:}h \Rightarrow c{:}(f\,g\,h) \in$ {Aa–b, Ma–b}:

$$d\psi_{1..m}{:}g \;\; e\psi_{m+1..n}{:}h \Rightarrow$$
$$c\psi_{1..n}{:}\lambda_{v_{1..n}} f\,(g\,v_{1..m})\,(h\,v_{m+1..n}) \quad \text{(Ac–d, Mc–d)}$$

Rules Ac–d and Mc–d stipulate non-local propagation through argument and modifier composition.

Inference rules for filler attachment apply gapped clauses to topicalized phrases as fillers. For $c \in C$, and $p \in P$:

$$p{:}g \;\; c\textbf{-g}p{:}h \Rightarrow c{:}\lambda_x \exists_y (g\,y) \wedge (h\,y\,x) \quad \text{(Fa)}$$

In contrast, Tse and Curran (2010) analyze the topic in non-movement topicalization as a sentential modifier, which gives 他 'he' in (6) the category S/S, serving as a sentential modifier for the sentence 胃口很好 'appetite is good.' This analysis conflates sentential adverbial modifiers such as 'today' with topics such as 'he' in (6), yielding incorrect dependencies and expending probability mass on ungrammatical derivations (e.g.with topics conjoined with adverbs).

3.5 Relative and appositive clauses

In Mandarin relative clauses, the particle 的 'de' takes a preceding clause containing a gap to form a relative clause modifying a succeeding noun. The modified noun is the filler of the gap in the relative clause. The inference rules for relative clauses apply the gapped *de*-clause to the modificand as a filler. For $c \in C$:

$$\textbf{D-g}c{:}g \;\; \textbf{N}{:}h \Rightarrow \textbf{N}{:}\lambda_x (h\,x) \wedge \exists_y (g\,x\,y) \quad \text{(R)}$$

A GCG analysis of a relative clause with an object gap is shown in (7).

(7) 'fish that cats eat'

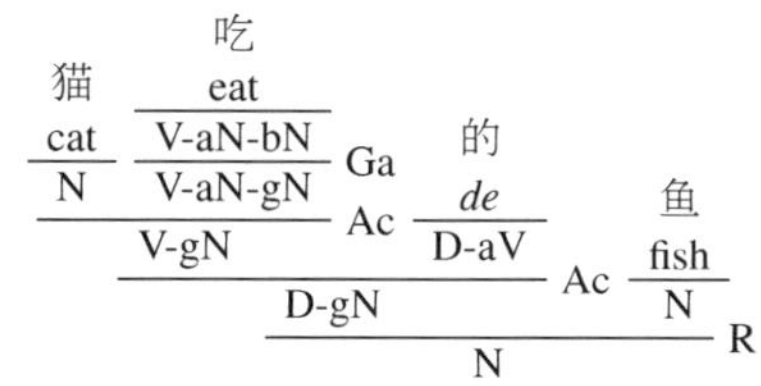

Our analysis of topicalization in (6) makes it easy to account for a relative clause which relativizes a topic. In (6) for example, relativizing the topic 他 'he' yields a nominal phrase containing a non-restrictive relative clause 胃口很好的他, 'he whose appetite is good.' A GCG analysis of this nominal phrase is shown in (8).

(8) 'he whose appetite is very good'

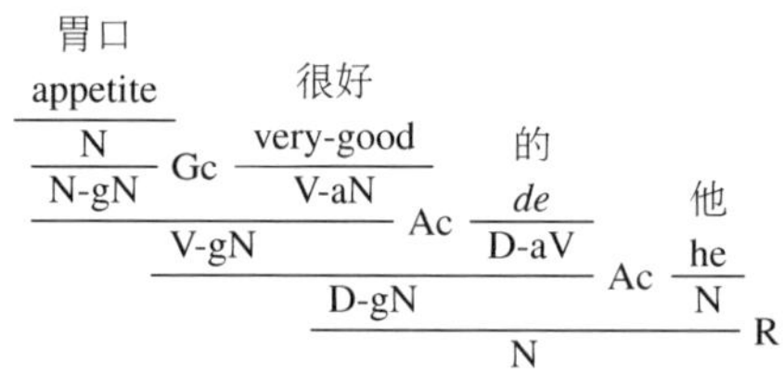

Appositive clauses in Mandarin Chinese are formed with the same 的 '*de*' particle used in relative clauses. However, unlike relative clauses, appositive clauses do not involve any gap constituent. In this GCG analysis of appositive clauses, 的 '*de*' receives the same category as it does in relative clauses. But the noun which takes an appositive clause as complement has the category **N-aD** to take a preceeding *de*-clause to further specify the content of the noun. An appositive clause in this grammar is shown in (9).

(9) 'the idea that high tech cannot be reached'

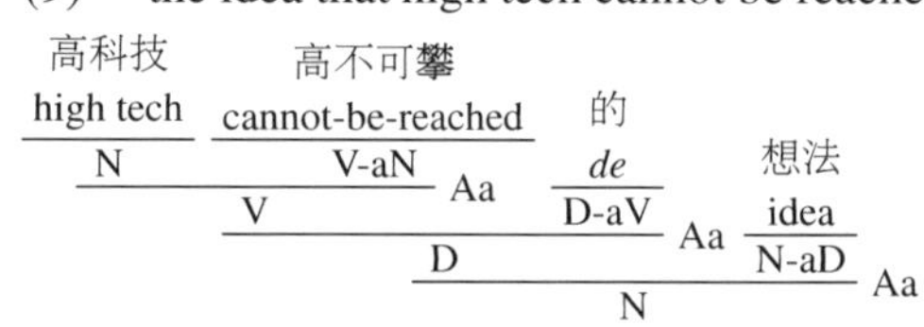

In the analyses described above, relative clauses with different types of gaps are differentiated, and relative clauses in general receive different analyses than appositive clauses. In the analysis of Tse and Curran (2010), a relative clause can only have either a subject or object gap in Chinese. Relative clauses that relativize topics receive the same categories as appositive clauses. This analysis blurs the distributional difference between certain types of relative clauses and appositive clauses, decreasing PCFG estimates of both types of relative clauses given the same (conflated) category.

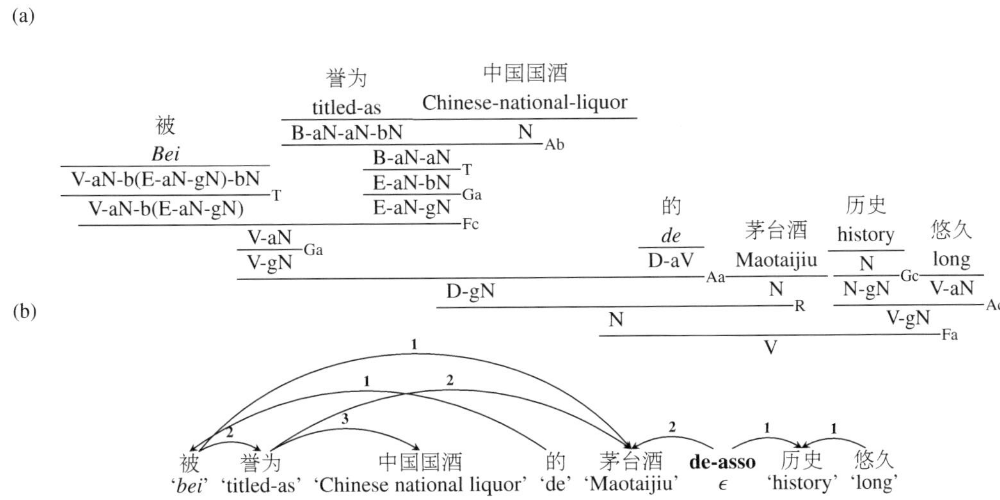

Figure 1: GCG derivation:"Maotaijiu, which is titled as the Chinese national liquor, has a long history" (a) and its associated dependencies (b)

3.6 *Ba* and *bei* constructions

Ba constructions in Mandarin Chinese require the affected patients of certain verbs to occur before the verb, instead of after the verb. For example, 鱼 'fish' in (10) is the object of 吃 'eat' and it occurs before the verb 'eat.' In the Penn Treebank, 把 *ba* takes a clause as argument. Therefore, 鱼吃了 'fish ate' in (10) is analyzed as a clausal complement of *ba*. This analysis makes 'fish' the subject of the verb 'eat,' instead of the object. Consequently, for example, Stanford dependencies extracted from Treebank annotations of this sentence have both 'nsubj (吃'eat,' 猫'cat')' and 'nsubj (吃'eat,' 鱼'fish'),' which is not correct.

(10) 'the cat ate the fish'

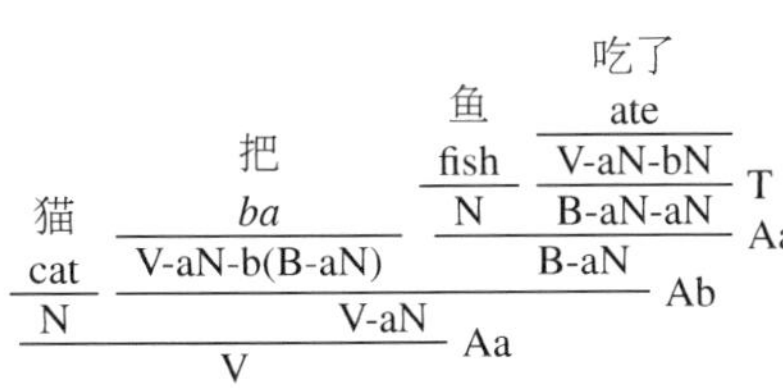

In our analysis, we propose that the particle *ba* takes a *ba*-verb as its complement. *Ba*-verbs are derived from transitive verbs with the type conversion rule given below.[5]

$$c{:}g \Rightarrow d{:}g \qquad \text{(T)}$$

Using the type conversion rule T, we change a transitive verb **V-aN-bN** to **B-aN-aN** to capture the fact that the verb that occurs within a *ba* construction takes a preceeding second argument.

The particle 把 *ba* is assigned the category **V-aN-b(B-aN)**, with coindexation between the referent of its subject ($\mathbf{f}_1\ x$) and the referent of the subject of its complement ($\mathbf{f}_1\ (\mathbf{f}_2\ x)$).

$$\text{把 'ba'} \mapsto \textbf{V-aN-b(B-aN)}{:}\lambda_x (\mathbf{f}_0\ x)=\mathsf{ba} \wedge (\mathbf{f}_1\ x)=(\mathbf{f}_1\ (\mathbf{f}_2\ x))$$

Usually, the affected patient is the direct object of a transitive verb, as shown in (10), but there are cases where some verbs can only occur in *ba* constructions or *bei* constructions. These types of verbs are *ba*-verbs to begin with and do not need to be changed from transitive verbs. They are given the general category **B-aN-aN-bN**. Many resultative verbs (VRD, in treebank annotation) have this category. An example is given in (11).

(11) 'We built Chongming into a port.'

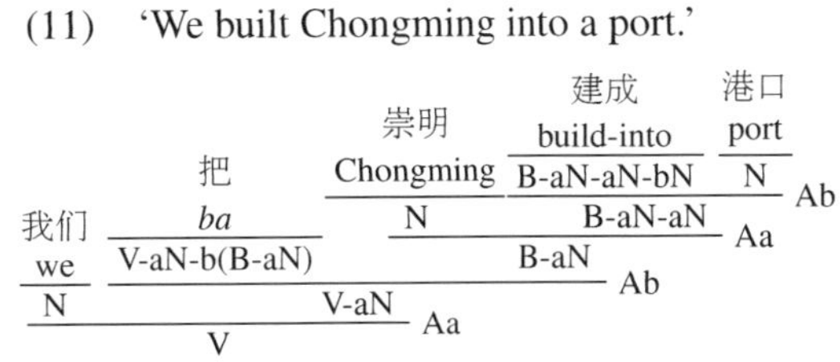

Mandarin Chinese uses the particle 被 *bei* to construct passive sentences. In *bei* constructions,

[5]This rule is constrained by fact that the function g is preserved, and its usage is constrained by parsing probabilities for particular categories. Following Featherston (2005) and Crocker and Keller (2005), the model described in this paper assumes that grammaticality judgements are gradient and determined by probabilities of compositional inferences occurring in the experience of a particular language user.

the patient argument of a verb, usually the second argument of a transitive verb or a *ba*-verb, is moved to the subject position of the clause. We propose the particle 被 *bei* takes a *bei*-verb as its complement. *Bei*-verbs, which are of the category **E-aN-gN**, are derived from **E-aN-bN** by introducing a gap by rule Ga. **E-aN-bN** is derived by the type conversion rule T from **V-aN-bN** or **B-aN-aN**, transitive verbs or *ba*-verbs. Here is the lexical entry we propose for the *bei* particle.

$$\text{被 'bei'} \mapsto \textbf{V-aN-b(E-aN-gN)-bN}: \lambda_x (\mathbf{f}_0\ x)=\mathsf{bei} \wedge (\mathbf{f}_3\ x)=(\mathbf{f}_1\ (\mathbf{f}_2\ x))$$

The lexical entry of 被 *bei* stipulates that the first argument of *bei* is the subject of its second argument, the VP complement, **E-aN-gN**. Since the agent in the passive voice construction is optional (as it is in passive voice in English), the category of the *bei* particle can have a type change from **V-aN-b(E-aN-gN)-bN** to **V-aN-b(E-aN-gN)**. The inference rule (Fc) is proposed for the composition of gap dependencies contained within succeeding arguments, where $p \in P$, $\varphi \in \{\textbf{-a},\textbf{-b}\} \times C$, and $\psi \in \{\textbf{-g}\} \times C$.

$$p\varphi_{1...n-1}\textbf{-b}(d\psi){:}g \quad d\psi{:}h \Rightarrow p\varphi{:}\lambda_x\, h\,(\mathbf{f}_1\, x)(\mathbf{f}_n\, x) \wedge g\, x \quad \text{(Fc)}$$

Using rule Fc, the first argument of the *bei* particle becomes the filler of the gap in the *bei* verb. This rule also supports an analysis of tough constructions in Chinese.

An example *bei*-construction which contains a transitive verb is shown in (12).

(12) 'The fish was eaten by the cat.'

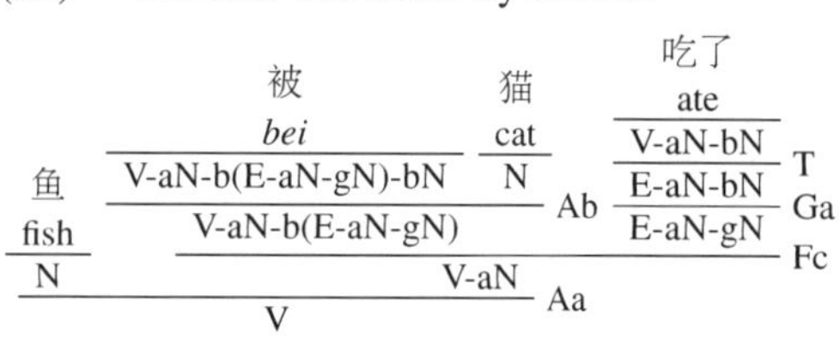

The Penn Treebank uses the category 'LB' for the *bei* particle where the optional agent argument occurs, and 'SB' for the *bei* particle where it is elided. Tse and Curran (2010) follow the Treebank annotation, proposing two different categories for the *bei* particle. For example the CCG category for 'LB' is $(S\backslash NP_y)/(S\backslash NP_x/NP_y)/NP_x$, in which a coindexation scheme is used to ensure that the subject of *bei* is coindexed with the object of its verbal complement. The *ba* particle, with the category $(S\backslash NP_y)/(S\backslash NP_y/NP_x)/NP_x$, is different from *bei* only in the coindexing scheme. However, if the passivized verb is not a transitive verb, such as 誉为 'titled-as' in Figure 1, it is hard to infer what the coindexing scheme should be like in the CCG analysis.

Figure 1 shows a GCG derivation of a sentence from the Chinese Treebank. We use this sentence to illustrate how topicalization, passive voice, and relative clauses are analyzed in the GCG framework and what kind of dependencies we can extract from GCG derivations.

4 Experiments

We use a set of reannotation rules similar to those described by Nguyen et al. (2012) to reannotate the Penn Chinese Treebank into GCG trees. These reannotation rules work within a perl script that traverses each bracketed sentence in the Penn Chinese Treebank by selecting each pair of matching brackets from the top of the tree to the bottom, then running a sed-like pattern substitution rule on each selection. With around 200 annotation rules, we currently fully annotate 71% of sentences (18,505 sentences out of 26,062) from the Penn Chinese Treebank 5 and 6.

In order to evaluate the Chinese GCG annotations in terms of parsing accuracy, we compare the parsing performance of a latent-variable parser trained on Chinese GCG annotations with that of the same parser trained on Chinese CCG annotations. The Chinese CCGbank is obtained by converting the Penn Chinese Treebank into CCG annotations according to Tse and Curran (2012).[6] We divided the fully annotated sentences in both grammars into training, development and test sections according to the section divisions suggested by Tse and Curran (2012). In order to have a better understanding of how the parsing performance changes with the size of the training data, we trained the Chinese CCG parser on both the full training set (ccg.full) and the same training set used for training the Chinese GCG parser (ccg.same). The detailed section divisions are shown in Table 1.

For the two CCG parsers, ccg.full and ccg.same, we use the Petrov and Klein (2007) latent variable PCFG trainer, with 5 split-merge cycles, which is the best setting indicated by Tse and Curran (2012). As with CCG, we ran the Petrov et al.

[6] https://github.com/jogloran/cnccgbank

Model	Train	Dev	Test
ccg.full	22680	689	1986
ccg.same	13677	689	1986
gcg	13677	689	1986

Table 1: Train/Dev/Test Split

	R	P	F	tag
ccg.same	78.64	78.96	78.80	85.62
ccg.full	80.69	81.13	80.91	87.24
gcg	82.70	83.86	83.28	93.65

Table 2: Parsing results on the development set

(2006) latent-variable PCFG trainer on the GCG-reannotated training corpus. The PCFG trainer was used 'off the shelf' and run with its default parameters, only varying the number of split-merge iterations on the development section. We found 5 split-merge iterations yielded the best parsing performance in the development section.

Tables 2 and 3 show the parsing performance of the parsers on the development and test sets. The parsing results show that a larger training set is beneficial to the parsing performance of the Chinese CCG parer; the parsing performance of the CCG parser trained on the full training set performs consistently better than the parser trained on 71% of the training set. The GCG parser, trained on 71% of the training set, seems to parse reasonably well even compared with the CCG parser trained on the full training set. It is worth noting that the GCG parser is much higher in tagging accuracy than the CCG parser, which supports our hypothesis that the CCG parser might suffer from sparse data problems.

However, direct comparison of the parsing performance of these two parsers is not fair because these two grammars define different categories and different tree structures. In order to ensure a fair comparison between these grammars, it is necessary to have them produce exactly the same target representation. In this experiment, we test the parsing performance of these two grammars on a common test set of sentences to which the two grammars assign the same tree structure when syntactic labels and unary branches are removed, see Figure 2. We found 984 sentences in the test set which have exactly the same unlabeled binary structures (Figure 2c) in both grammars.

Table 4 shows the parsing results (F1) on parses with both syntactic category labels and unary branches removed (NoUnary+NoLab). After re-

	R	P	F	tag
ccg.same	78.39	78.55	78.47	85.02
ccg.full	79.77	79.93	79.85	86.33
gcg	82.19	83.07	82.63	93.66

Table 3: Parsing results on the test set

		% Err. Reduct. vs.		p-value vs.	
	F1	ccg.same	ccg.full	ccg.same	ccg.full
ccg.same	88.76	–	–	–	–
ccg.full	89.39	–	–	–	–
gcg	**90.07**	11.65	6.409	0.0007	0.04

Table 4: Parsing results, error reduction ratios and significance testing results on the common test set of NoUnary+NoLab trees.

moving unary branches, the parses have exclusively binary tree structures and have identical results for precision, recall and F1 in parsing evaluations. Since both grammars predict exactly the same binary tree structures with exactly the same ('X') categories, significance testing is performed on these predictions using bootstrap resampling.

Results in Table 4 show that the parsing performance of the Petrov and Klein (2007) parser trained on the GCG-reannotated corpus is more accurate with strong significance ($p < 0.001$) than the same parser trained on the CCG-reannotated corpus of the same size. We observe a significant improvement ($p < 0.05$) of the GCG parser over the CCG parser trained on the full training set.

We believe that the Chinese CCG parser suffers from data sparsity effects. Excluding those words which are only associated with one preterminal category, the lexical-categorial confusion rate is 3.45 for the Chinese CCG annotations and 2.59 for the Chinese GCG annotations, which is also reflected in the large gap (more than 5 points) between their tagging accuracy. Enforcing a small set of language-independent inference rules in the Chinese CCG-annotations might have some formal appeal, but it leads to a large set of syntactic categories, many of which, such as nominal or adverbial modifiers, are syntactically or semantically indistinguishable. Since the GCG described in this paper uses a larger set of inference rules and consequently fewer category labels, it suffers fewer sparse data effects.

5 Conclusion and discussion

This paper has described a generalized categorial grammar for Mandarin Chinese, reannotated

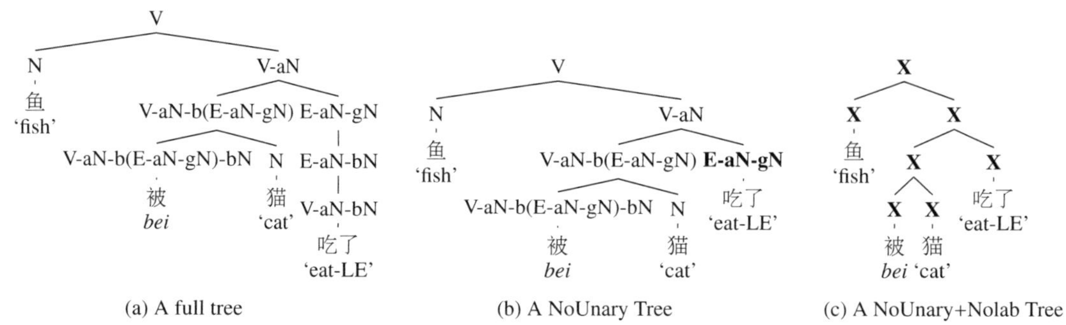

Figure 2: Constructing common test set

from the Penn Chinese Treebank. Unlike previous efforts using strongly lexicalized CCG (Tse and Curran, 2010), the reannotated corpus described in this paper adopts a policy of moderate lexicalization, allowing both inference rules and lexical categories to be language-specific. This moderation offers considerable representational freedom, particularly in modeling Chinese *ba*-, *bei*-, and *de*-constructions, which make substantial use of unbounded dependencies. Experimental results appear to show that, while there may be some formal appeal to a small universal set of language-independent combinators (Steedman, 2000; Steedman, 2002; Steedman, 2012), the large category set resulting from it might impose an empirical cost for parsing tasks.

The reannotation rules are available at `http://www.sourceforge.net/projects/modelblocks`.

References

Keith Allan. 1977. Classfiers. *Language*, 53:285–311.

Emmon Bach. 1981. Discontinuous constituents in generalized categorial grammars. *Proceedings of the Annual Meeting of the Northeast Linguistic Society (NELS)*, 11:1–12.

Hagit Borer. 2005. *Structure sense*. Oxford.

Matthew W. Crocker and Frank Keller. 2005. Probabilistic grammars as models of gradience in language processing. In Gisbert Fanselow, Caroline Féry, Ralph Vogel, and Matthias Schlesewsky, editors, *GRADIENCE IN GRAMMAR: GENERATIVE PERSPECTIVES*. University Press.

Sam Featherston. 2005. Universals and grammaticality: wh-constraints in German and English. *Linguistics*, 43(4):667–711.

Lauri Karttunen. 1989. Radical lexicalism. In M. R. Baltin and A. S. Kroch, editors, *Alternative Conceptions of Phrase Structure*, pages 43–65. University of Chicago Press, Chicago.

Jonathan K. Kummerfeld, Daniel Tse, James R. Curran, and Dan Klein. 2013. An empirical examination of challenges in chinese parsing. In *Proceedings of ACL'13*, pages 98–103, Sofia, Bulgaria.

Luan Nguyen, Marten van Schijndel, and William Schuler. 2012. Accurate unbounded dependency recovery using generalized categorial grammars. In *Proceedings of COLING '12*, pages 2125–2140, Mumbai, India.

Richard T. Oehrle. 1994. Term-labeled categorial type systems. *Linguistics and Philosophy*, 17(6):633–678.

Slav Petrov and Dan Klein. 2007. Improved inference for unlexicalized parsing. In *Proceedings of NAACL HLT 2007*, pages 404–411, Rochester, New York, April. Association for Computational Linguistics.

Slav Petrov, Leon Barrett, Romain Thibaux, and Dan Klein. 2006. Learning accurate, compact, and interpretable tree annotation. In *Proceedings of COLING/ACL'06*.

Laura Rimell, Stephen Clark, and Mark Steedman. 2009. Unbounded dependency recovery for parser evaluation. In *Proceedings of EMNLP 2009*, volume 2, pages 813–821.

William Schuler and Adam Wheeler. 2014. Cognitive compositional semantics using continuation dependencies. In *Third Joint Conference on Lexical and Computational Semantics (*SEM'14)*.

Mark Steedman. 2000. *The syntactic process*. MIT Press/Bradford Books, Cambridge, MA.

Mark Steedman. 2002. Plans, affordances, and combinatory grammar. *Linguistics and Philosophy*, 25.

Mark Steedman. 2012. *Taking Scope - The Natural Semantics of Quantifiers*. MIT Press.

Daniel Tse and James R. Curran. 2010. Chinese CCGbank: extracting CCG derivations from the penn chinese treebank. In *Proceedings of COLING '10*, pages 1083–1091.

Daniel Tse and James R. Curran. 2012. The Challenges of Parsing Chinese with Combinatory Categorial Grammar. In *Proceedings of NAACL-HLT '12*, pages 295–304, Montréal, Canada.

Nianwen Xue, Fei Xian, Fu-Dong Chiou, and Martha Palmer. 2005. The Penn Chinese Treebank: Phrase Structure annotation of a large corpus. *Natural Language Engineering*, 11:207–238.

Orthography Engineering in Grammatical Framework

Krasimir Angelov
University of Gothenburg
krasimir@chalmers.se

Abstract

Orthography is an integral part of language but in grammar engineering it is often ignored, simplified or just delegated to external tools. We present new extensions to Grammatical Framework, which allow one and the same formalism to describe both orthography, syntax and morphology. These extensions are also easily generalizable to other formalisms.

1 Introduction

Orthography is often assumed to be something simple that is easily delegated to pre- or post-processors. The real grammar engineering starts only after the tokenization.

Unfortunately if this is mostly true for English, it is more complicated in other languages. For instance, most Germanic languages tend to build compound nouns composed of one or more simple nouns. Furthermore German requires that nouns should start with a capital letter unless if the noun is in the second part of a compound. Handling compounds requires a separate compound splitter (Koehn and Knight, 2003) for parsing and proper generator in linearization. The capitalization is usually ignored in parsing but must be recovered for generation (Lita et al., 2003; Chelba and Acero, 2004).

Agglutinative languages tend to build long words by adding more and more suffixes which blurs the borderline between word and morpheme. In that case the words themselves need to be parsed since it is not possible to enumerate all word forms in a finite lexicon. The extreme case is in languages that does not separate words with spaces at all. This is usually solved by using a preprocessor that finds a lattice of possible word segmentations which are later parsed (Chappelier et al., 1999; Hall, 2005).

Finally, in many languages there are lexical units that are phonetically dependent on the context. A typical example is the indefinite article *a/an* in English which is different depending on the next word in the sentence. Similarly the definite article *la/l* in French depends on the next word, except that the correct resolution also requires knowledge of a syntactic context which is available only in the grammar.

Because of all these complications, delegating the orthography to an external tool has many engineering disadvantages. To start with, a new tool has to be developed for every language. The tool moreover should partly encode knowledge that is already in the grammar. For instance for compound splitting the tool should have access to the lexicon of the grammar. When an application is ported from one platform to another then the grammar itself is usually stored in a portable format and only the grammar interpreter needs to be ported. However if external pre- and post-processors are used then they have to be ported as well. Everything is a lot simpler if the orthography is encoded in a portable way as part of the grammar itself.

We present extensions to the Grammatical Framework (GF; Ranta 2011) which allow orthographic conventions to be encoded as an integral part of the grammar. This possess the following challenges.

First of all GF is a reversible formalism. One and the same grammar is used for both parsing and generation. In parsing we want grammars that are robust and permissible as long as this does not produce incorrect analyses. On the other hand in generation we want to produce text of the best possible shape. This means for instance that accepting a German noun that is not capitalized can be desirable but generating a text where the nouns are not capitalized should be avoided.

GF is by design a multilingual formalism. A

Proceedings of the Grammar Engineering Across Frameworks (GEAF) Workshop, 53rd Annual Meeting of the ACL and 7th IJCNLP, pages 33–40,
Beijing, China, July 26-31, 2015. ©2015 Association for Computational Linguistics

single grammar typically contains modules for several different languages. The modules are linked together through a Logical Framework[1] (Harper et al., 1993) which serves as a language independent abstract syntax. In this multilingual setting, having different pre- or post-processors for the different languages will defeat the purpose of having a single multilingual grammar.

GF grammars are distributed in a portable format (Angelov et al., 2010) which can be deployed in different environments ranging from web servers and desktop translation systems to mobile devices. The virtual machine for GF (Angelov, 2011) is also developed as a platform independent software. By adding the orthographic extensions to the framework itself, we automatically make more GF applications portable since they will not be dependent on external tools.

The grammarian in GF writes a grammar by using a high-level functional programming language reminiscent of Haskell and ML. However, if we abstract away from the high-level features, the backbone of the framework (Ljunglöf, 2004) is equivalent to a Parallel Multiple Context-Free Grammar (PMCFG; Seki et al. 1991). The latter subsumes other popular formalisms such as TAG (Joshi and Schabes, 1997) and CCG (Steedman, 2000) but contains only some of the possible RCG grammars (Boullier, 1998). The full logical framework embedded in GF in principle makes GF as expressive as HPSG (Pollard and Sag, 1994) and other unification grammars, but we often find this extra level of complexity unnecessary and we stick with the backbone of the framework.

The extensions that we present are mostly framework independent and they can be added even to simple context-free grammars. Because of that and to make it easier to relate the extensions to other formalisms we will use context-free grammars for the rest of the paper. The actual implementation is in the PMCFG engine behind GF.

There are four groups of extensions that we present in four sections:

- `BIND`, `SOFT_BIND` and `SOFT_SPACE` in Section 2
- `CAPIT` and `ALL_CAPIT` in Section 3
- `pre` in Section 4
- `nonExist` in Section 5

[1]The name Grammatical Framework (GF) itself is the analogy of the general Logical Framework in Harper et al.

All of these extensions were frequently requested by different people in the GF community. They are now available as primitive operations of type string (`Str`) and are exported from the standard module `Prelude`. The only exception is `pre`, which is a complex programming language construction. In a public application the extensions were first extensively used in the offline mobile translator for twelve languages developed in Angelov et al. (2014).

2 Controlling the Spaces

The first problem is to decide whether and when to put spaces between words. Like all formalisms, GF describes a language as a set of strings over a finite set of terminal symbols. This is problematic in agglutinative languages and languages with compound words since their vocabulary is theoretically infinite.

The solution is to redefine what is considered a word in the language. For instance, a Swedish grammar should treat compound words such as *datavetenskap* 'computer science' as two separate words *data* and *vetenskap*, which, following the orthographic convention in Swedish, are written without space in between. The grammar encodes that the two words are bound together by inserting a special token called BIND. This can be exemplified with a rule like:

```
fun CompoundN : N -> N -> N
lin CompoundN n1 n2 =
          n1 ++ BIND ++ n2
```

Where `CompoundN` combines the two nouns referred by the two variables `n1` and `n2` into a single compound noun. Obviously a realistic rule will be more complicated but the example captures the essense. The operator ++ specifies that we combine words together to build a phrase. We put the nouns one after another but we also insert `BIND` to indicate that there is no space in-between. The result from:

```
CompoundN data_N vetenskap_N
```

is the compound *datavetenskap*. In contrast if we had missed the `BIND`, we would generate *data␣vetenskap* which is not the correct Swedish spelling. Both the types of the arguments as well as the type of the result is noun (`N`), which allows for compounds with multiple components with alternative associativities.

	0	1...∞	0...∞
0	BIND	*	SOFT_BIND
1	*		SOFT_SPACE

Table 1: Tokens for controlling the spacing. The column shows how many spaces the parser will accept and the row shows how many spaces are put by the generator. Inconsistent combinations are marked with $*$.

The same mechanism makes it possible to model agglutinative languages. There we use a finite lexicon of words but we are free to add suffixes syntactically. The suffixes are attached by using `BIND` which prevents the insertion of unnecessary spaces. This has been used extensively in Finnish where the lexicon is composed of stems and suffixes while the words are composed syntactically. To a lesser extend the same technique is also applied in Estonian (Listenmaa and Kaljurand, 2014) and Maltese (Camilleri, 2013).

`BIND` is useful even in English. For example the grammars for all languages including English must parse numerals in order to recognize whether the numerals require singular or plural noun, i.e. "1 apple" but "2 apples". When we have numerals with more than one digit then the grammar must use `BIND` to glue individual digits together.

A related issue is that in many languages the punctuation signs are glued to the previous word (or the next word for opening parenthesis). Here we could use `BIND` as well but this means that the parser would reject sentences where the punctuation is separated. Usually we do not want this and for that purpose we also introduced `SOFT_BIND`. In generation, `BIND` and `SOFT_BIND` are identical, but in parsing, the latter allows optional spaces between the surrounding words.

For completeness we also added `SOFT_SPACE` – a token which in generation mode leaves space between the surrounding words but in parsing allows the space to be omitted. The three spacing tokens are summarized in Table 1. The rows show how many spaces are inserted in generation and the columns how many spaces are accepted in parsing. Two of the combinations are inconsistent since this would generate sentences that are impossible to parse. One combination corresponds to the default case where ++ is used alone and the rest of the combinations are represented with a special token.

It should be obvious by now how `BIND` can be implemented in the natural language generator. When we see `BIND` then we just glue the next word to the previous one. The implementation in the parser is not so obvious. We use a parsing algorithm (Angelov, 2009) which is a variant of Earley (1968) but is generalised to PMCFG.

Earley's algorithm maintains items like:

$$[^j_i \mathrm{A} \rightarrow \alpha \bullet \beta] \quad (1)$$

which encode the fact that the rule $\mathrm{A} \rightarrow \alpha\beta$ has been partly recognized between positions i and j in the input sentence. The difference in a parser which can handle bindings is that positions i and j must be measured in number of characters rather than number of words. Now if the parser encounters an item like:

$$[^i_i \mathrm{N} \rightarrow \bullet \text{"data" BIND "vetenskap"}] \quad (2)$$

and the current word is *datavetenskap* then it generates a new item:

$$[^{i+4}_i \mathrm{N} \rightarrow \text{"data"} \bullet \text{BIND "vetenskap"}] \quad (3)$$

The items in the original Earley algorithm are grouped in sets with exactly one set for every position between two words. In our implementation there could be from zero to two sets for every character position. Typically there is one set for every position that corresponds to a space between two words, i.e. exactly like in the original algorithm. However, item 3 for example will force a new set to be generated for the position between `data` and `vetenskap`. This state is marked in a special way since there is no space at that position. The only tokens that make it possible to exit from this state are `BIND`, `SOFT_BIND` and `SOFT_SPACE`. This is exactly what will happen with item 3 which will lead to the item:

$$[^{i+4}_i \mathrm{N} \rightarrow \text{"data" BIND} \bullet \text{"vetenskap"}] \quad (4)$$

The new item ends at the same position but now it will be put in a new state which is not marked as special and this will make it possible to accept *vetenskap* as a next token.

Exactly the same modification to the Earley algorithm is also applicable to the PMCFG parser which is the basis of the implementation in GF. Note that unlike Chappelier et al. (1999) and Hall (2005), we do not need a lattice to represent the ambiguous word segmentation. The ambiguity is naturally represented as different alternatives in the parse chart. However, the advantage of the lattice is that a word is segmented only if all parts are possible parts of the lexicon. In contrast the naive implementation of a parser with `BIND` would segment out a prefix even if the rest of the word is not a possible word. This is easily resolved by using limited lookahead in the parser.

3 Controlling the Capitalization

Compounds in German require both gluing words together as well as altering the capitalization. For example from the nouns *Aktion* and *Plan* we build *Aktionsplan* where the second noun is lower-cased. This means that for every noun we need one form where the first letter is capitalized, and another where it is not. The same applies also to verbs since all verbs can be nominalized. For example from *laufen* 'walk' we get *das Laufen* 'walking' which requires capitalization.

Instead of storing each word form twice in the lexicon, it is advantageous to have a way to dynamically control the capitalization. We can achieve this by introducing one more special token which we call `CAPIT`. The effect of `CAPIT` is that it causes the next word in the sentence to be rendered with initial upper case letter. We store the words in the lexicon in lower case, but by inserting `CAPIT` in the right places in the grammar we guarantee the right capitalization.

In a very simplified form, it could be written like this:

```
fun UseN : N -> CN
lin UseN n = CAPIT ++ n
```

Here `UseN` is a function which converts a noun into a common noun. Just like with `CompoundN`, here, we ignore case, agreement and other irrelevant grammatical features. The noun can be a simple noun as well as a compound (composed by using `CompoundN`), and it is always in lower-case. We add `CAPIT` in front of it to alter the capitalization.

Altering the capitalization is the behaviour of `CAPIT` in generation mode. In parsing we would like to have robust processing, even if the input sentence does not have the correct capitalization. By default the GF parser is case sensitive but by adding in the top module of the corresponding language the declaration:

```
flags
  case_sensitive=off;
```

we can instruct the parser to lower-case the input before parsing. If all words in the grammar are lower-cased too, the parsing becomes case insensitive. This demands also that the parser must simply ignore `CAPIT`. In an Earley style parser, this corresponds to adding the rule:

$$\frac{[_i^j\ \mathrm{A} \rightarrow \alpha \bullet \mathrm{CAPIT}\ \beta]}{[_i^j\ \mathrm{A} \rightarrow \alpha\ \mathrm{CAPIT} \bullet \beta]} \quad (5)$$

i.e. every time when we encounter an item with a dot before `CAPIT` we are simply allowed to move the dot to the next position.

The requirement that all words in the grammar must be lower-cased contradicts the already established convention for defining lexical entries in German. An entry is defined by applying a smart paradigm function (Détrez and Ranta, 2012) to one or more word forms:

```
mkN "Junge" "Jungen" masculine
```

Here the forms are expected to be the lexicographic forms used in the traditional paper dictionaries. Since the tradition is to use the capitalized forms, the same convention was adopted in the GF grammar as well. The conflict was easily resolved by changing the definition of the paradigm function `mkN`. Because it is computed at compile time, it has more freedom and it internally lower-cases the forms listed in the definition.

German was the primary motivation for adding `CAPIT`, but the robustness with respect to the capitalization is another aspect which is also useful in other languages. One prototypical use is the capitalization of the first word in a sentence. Another example is English which has a number of words (compass directions, country adjectives, etc.) that by convention are spelled with upper case. In all those examples if they are encoded with `CAPIT` then parsing succeeds even if the capitalization is wrong.

The requirement that all lexical entries in the grammar must be in lower-case means that we need special treatment for acronyms which are typically written with capital letters. Using `CAPIT` would be enough, if we split those into a sequence of letters glued with `BIND`. For example IT (information technology) can be encoded as:

```
          CAPIT ++ "i" ++
BIND ++ CAPIT ++ "t"
```

The same trick works even for mixed case combinations like the word LaTeX. However, using the trick requires a tedious and verbose encoding. It is acceptable for rare combinations like LaTeX, but we want a more compact solution for the normal acronyms. For that purpose we also added `ALL_CAPIT`. The behaviour of `ALL_CAPIT` is that it capitalizes all letters in the next orthographic word instead of only the first one. It is important to emphasize that `ALL_CAPIT` applies to the next orthographic word and not to the next grammatical word. This means that if `ALL_CAPIT` is followed by a sequence of words glued with `BIND` or `SOFT_BIND` then the whole sequence will be capitalized.

Finally we should note that the robustness in the parser also introduces additional spurious ambiguities. For instance the acronym IT becomes indistinguishable from the pronoun *it*. There should be a soft preference for the pronoun, if the word is spelled with lower-case, and alternatively in the other direction if the word is upper-cased. This is easy to implement in a parser which computes weights for alternative analyses. In that case additional weight must be added to every analysis that needs Rule 5 and where the next word in the sentence has the wrong capitalization.

4 Phonetic Dependencies

It is quite common to have words in the language whose exact form depends on the next word. Typical examples are the indefinite article a/an in English, the definite articles le/l', la/l' in French, and the prepositions s/săs and v/văv in Bulgarian. Keeping track of the form of the next word in the grammar is tedious and error-prone. It is much easier to delay the choice until we know all words in the sentence. At that phase it is easy to check the next word.

We do this by using the `pre` token[2]. Its general syntax is:

```
pre {default;
      form1 / prefixes1;
      ...
      formN / prefixesN}
```

Here we start with the default form which applies if there is no more specific variant. After the default are the specific cases. Every case is a word form followed by slash and a list of prefixes. If the next word after `pre` starts with one of the prefixes in the list then the final sentence will contain the corresponding word form. In case of ambiguity the first matching alternative is selected.

Both the default and each of the specific forms are arbitrary expressions. They could for instance consist of multiple orthographic words, or they could include other special tokens such as `BIND`. The definite article in French is a good example:

```
pre {"la"; "l'" ++ BIND / voyelle}
```

If the next word starts with a vowel then the article *la* should be contracted to *l'* and the contraction should be attached to the next word. We specify this by using the expression `voyelle` which is defined as the list of all vowels in French. *l'* is followed by `BIND` to indicate that there is no space before the next word. The default is *la* without `BIND` since it is spelled as a separate word.

The above gives the false impression that contraction in French is fully implemented. Unfortunately this is not exactly the case. The problem is that the aspirated h in French does not allow contraction while the non-aspirated h demands it. Unfortunately it is not possible to find whether h is aspirated by just looking at the prefix of the word. For this we need to know the whole word. There is a similar problem in English where in order to choose a/an we need to know whether the next word is pronounced with initial vowel. Unfortunately this is not always possible to infer from the orthographic prefix of the word. For that reason the implementation for phonetic dependencies in English and French is only approximate in the current grammars. In contrast, the prepositions s/săs and v/văv in Bulgarian are always reliably detected since the orthography and the phonetics in Bulgarian match very well. A better implementation for English and French would require a grammar that models in parallel both the orthography and the phonetics of the language. In that case `pre` should refer to the phonetic form of the next word rather than to the orthographic form.

French has one more feature which illustrates why orthography should not be implemented outside of the grammar. The problem is that the definite article *le* in combination with the preposition *de* is contracted to *du*, i.e.:

Le livre du garçon

instead of:

Le livre de le garçon

At the same time *le* is also the pronoun *it* which

[2]Strictly speaking `pre` is not a new addition to GF, but its operational behaviour was never precisely defined. It also interacts with the orthographic extensions, so it deserves attention in the current paper.

does not allow the same contraction here:

Il m'a dit de le faire

This is easy to implement in the grammar by using the syntactic context, but it is difficult to resolve in a post processor working only with the surface form of the final sentence.

`pre` is also used in the generation of punctuation. The problem is that in many languages non-restrictive relative clauses are separated from the rest of the sentence with commas before and after the clause. However, the closing comma should be used only if there is no other punctuation mark and if the comma is not the last word in the sentence. The right way to encode this is:

```
pre {"";
     "" / punct;
     SOFT_BIND ++ "," / ""}
```

Here the first special case uses the expression `punct` which lists all punctuation symbols. This means that if the word after the comma is punctuation, then we just generate the empty string. The second case uses empty string as a prefix for filtering. By definition, an empty prefix matches only if there is at least one word after `pre`. Obviously the empty string is a valid prefix for every possible word. But, if there is no following word then only the default form is applicable. We used the empty string as the default since this is what we want to generate if we are at the end of the sentence. Finally, the use of `SOFT_BIND` in the expression ensures that comma is glued to the preceding word in the sentence.

In generation mode, we always propagate the `pre` until we know all words in the sentence and then we replace it with the correct alternative. In parsing we decided that we want to accept all alternatives regardless of whether they agree with the constraints. Usually this does not lead to false ambiguities and accepting more alternatives only makes the parser more robust.

5 Degenerate Inflection Tables

Another issue, that is not really related to orthography, but is also easily solved by adding special kinds of tokens in the grammar, is when a word has missing inflection form. The problem is that every lexical entry in GF is not a single word but an inflection table with all possible forms. The grammarian defines the entry by applying a smart paradigm function, which is computed to an inflection table. For example if we define:

```
lin apple_N = mkN "apple"
```

the result will be something similar to:

```
lin apple_N =
      table {Sg => "apple";
             Pl => "apples"}
```

This representation fails for degenerate words that miss one or more forms. For that purpose we introduced the token `nonExist`. It can be used in any place where a word should be put but the actual language does not have the appropriate form.

In generation mode, `nonExist` behaves like an exception. Any attempt to linearise a sentence which contains `nonExist` will fail completely and no output will be generated. Ideally the grammarian should avoid exceptional situations and write grammars that always produce sensible output. At least this should be the goal for expressions generated from the intended start category, i.e. for sentences. Avoiding the exceptions is usually possible by using parameters to control the possible choices in the grammar. `nonExist` is still useful as an explicit marker for impossible combinations in nested categories, i.e. categories that are not used as start categories. If hiding all exceptions in the grammar is not possible then at least by using `nonExist` the user gets a chance to handle the situation by rephrasing the request.

`nonExist` interacts in an interesting way with variants in the grammar. GF provides the bar (|) operator for listing alternative linearisations. For example `a | b` is an expression which lists the two expressions `a` and `b` as two different alternatives. The API to the GF runtime provides methods for computing all possible alternatives for one and the same expression. In that case if one of the alternatives includes `nonExist` then it is simply filtered out. Using variants in combination with `nonExist` is yet another way to hide exceptions.

In parsing mode `nonExist` is implemented by simply stating that items like this:

$$[^j_i\ A \rightarrow \alpha \bullet \texttt{nonExist}\ \beta]$$

should not lead to any further derivations. A hacked-up version of `nonExist` can be implemented by defining it as a special word which is usually not used in the target language. In this way we can hope that the special word will never appear in an actual sentence and this will give us the intended behaviour. However, this is first of all inelegant and second it will become visible from some of the API calls. For example GF is commonly used for designing controlled languages where the parser is used inside authoring tools to assist the user in writing valid phrases in the language. In that case using the hack will cause the special token to show up in the suggestions from the authoring tool. Instead we implemented `nonExist` as a parser internal operation which is always invisible from the API calls.

6 Conclusion and Future Work

We presented a number of extensions in GF that make it easier to model orthographic phenomena without the need to use external pre- and post-processors. Keeping all the grammatical knowledge in a single framework is a definite engineering advantage that gave us knowledge sharing and portability. All of the extensions were extensively tested in practice as part of the translation system demonstrated in Angelov et al. (2014).

In the design we assumed two conflicting requirements: high-precision in generation and robustness in parsing. This sounds like a logical choice for most applications. It is possible, however, that for some applications, a more strict parser will be desirable, too. For example in an application for checking the correctness of a sentence we may want to be more strict. There are two ways in which this can be achieved. First of all it is always possible to use the robust parser for parsing the original input. After that the analysis can be fed back to the generator which will produce the canonical linearisation. The input can be compared with the canonical linearisation to identify potential problems. Another more involved solution is that we can extend the parser to keep record of all cases where some constraint has been violated. In that way after the parsing is finished, the user could consult the list of cases.

There is one more issue for which we have not made a firm decision yet. We have already mentioned several times the ++ operator which puts two phrases together. The framework has also an operator + which is similar but does not insert a space between the phrases. Its behaviour is similar to the combination ++ `BIND` ++ except that it is computed at compile time rather than at runtime. Currently its primary use is to compute new inflection forms in the definitions for different morphological operations. In principle, we could extend its use to a runtime operator which will further fuse the boundary between grammatical and orthographic words. Whether or not this is a good design decision is still not clear to us. In any case extending the domain of + would not make the use of `BIND` obsolete since `BIND` can also interact in a non trivial way with `pre` as in the French example. There are also similar examples in Catalan and Maltese.

Acknowledgement

Thanks to Aarne Ranta and the annonymous reviewers for their useful comments on the earlier draft of the paper. Swedish Research Council (Vetenskapsrådet) has supported this work under grant number 2012-4506.

References

Krasimir Angelov, Björn Bringert, and Aarne Ranta. 2010. PGF: A Portable Run-Time Format for Type-Theoretical Grammars. *Journal of Logic, Language and Information*, 19:201–228.

Krasimir Angelov, Aarne Ranta, and Björn Bringert. 2014. Speech-enabled hybrid multilingual translation for mobile devices. In *European Chapter of the Association for Computational Linguistics*, Gothenburg.

Krasimir Angelov. 2009. Incremental parsing with parallel multiple context-free grammars. In *European Chapter of the Association for Computational Linguistics*.

Krasimir Angelov. 2011. *The Mechanics of the Grammatical Framework*. Ph.D. thesis, Chalmers University of Technology.

Pierre Boullier. 1998. A proposal for a natural language processing syntactic backbone. Technical Report 3342, INRIA.

John J. Camilleri. 2013. A Computational Grammar and Lexicon for Maltese. Master's thesis, Chalmers University of Technology, Gothenburg, Sweden, September.

J.-C. Chappelier, M. Rajman, R. Arages, and A. Rozenknop. 1999. Lattice parsing for speech recognition. In *In Proceedings of 6me*, pages 95–104.

Ciprian Chelba and Alex Acero, 2004. *Proceedings of the 2004 Conference on Empirical Methods in Natural Language Processing*, chapter Adaptation of Maximum Entropy Capitalizer: Little Data Can Help a Lo.

Grégoire Détrez and Aarne Ranta. 2012. Smart paradigms and the predictability and complexity of inflectional morphology. In *Proceedings of the 13th Conference of the European Chapter of the Association for Computational Linguistics*, EACL '12, pages 645–653, Stroudsburg, PA, USA. Association for Computational Linguistics.

Jay Clark Earley. 1968. *An Efficient Context-free Parsing Algorithm*. Ph.D. thesis, Carnegie Mellon University, Pittsburgh, PA, USA. AAI6907901.

Keith B. Hall. 2005. *Best-first Word-lattice Parsing: Techniques for Integrated Syntactic Language Modeling*. Ph.D. thesis, Providence, RI, USA. AAI3174615.

Robert Harper, Furio Honsell, and Gordon Plotkin. 1993. A framework for defining logics. *J. ACM*, 40:143–184, January.

Aravind Joshi and Yves Schabes. 1997. Tree-adjoining grammars. In Grzegorz Rozenberg and Arto Salomaa, editors, *Handbook of Formal Languages. Vol 3: Beyond Words*, chapter 2, pages 69–123. Springer-Verlag, Berlin/Heidelberg/New York.

Philipp Koehn and Kevin Knight. 2003. Empirical methods for compound splitting. In *Proceedings of the Tenth Conference on European Chapter of the Association for Computational Linguistics - Volume 1*, EACL '03, pages 187–193, Stroudsburg, PA, USA. Association for Computational Linguistics.

Inari Listenmaa and Kaarel Kaljurand. 2014. Computational estonian grammar in grammatical framework. In *Proceedings of LREC 2014*, pages 13–18.

Lucian Vlad Lita, Abe Ittycheriah, Salim Roukos, and Nanda Kambhatla. 2003. truecasing. In *Proceedings of the 41st Annual Meeting on Association for Computational Linguistics - Volume 1*, ACL '03, pages 152–159, Stroudsburg, PA, USA. Association for Computational Linguistics.

Peter Ljunglöf. 2004. *Expressivity and Complexity of the Grammatical Framework*. Ph.D. thesis, Department of Computer Science, Gothenburg University and Chalmers University of Technology, November.

Carl Jess Pollard and Ivan A. Sag. 1994. *Head-driven phrase structure grammar*. Studies in contemporary linguistics. Center for the study of language and information Chicago (Ill.) London, Stanford (Calif.).

Aarne Ranta. 2011. *Grammatical Framework: Programming with Multilingual Grammars*. CSLI Publications, Stanford. ISBN-10: 1-57586-626-9 (Paper), 1-57586-627-7 (Cloth).

Hiroyuki Seki, Takashi Matsumura, Mamoru Fujii, and Tadao Kasami. 1991. On multiple context-free grammars. *Theoretical Computer Science*, 88(2):191–229, October.

Mark Steedman. 2000. *The syntactic process*. MIT Press, Cambridge, MA, USA.

A Cloud-Based Editor for Multilingual Grammars

Thomas Hallgren **Ramona Enache** **Aarne Ranta**
Department of Computer Science and Engineering
Chalmers University of Technology and University of Gothenburg
hallgren@chalmers.se ramona.enache@chalmers.se aarne@chalmers.se

Abstract

Writing deep linguistic grammars has been considered a highly specialized skill, requiring the use of tools with steep learning curves and complex installation procedures. As the use of statistical methods has increased, new generations of computational linguists are getting less and less prepared for grammar writing tasks. In an aim to provide a better learning experience for grammar writers, we present a grammar engineering tool that resides in the cloud. It has been used in several tutorial courses and self-studies, and it allows absolute beginners to write their first grammars and parse examples in 10 minutes. The cloud-based grammar engineering tool is built on top of GF (Grammatical Framework), a grammar formalism that has an explicit tecto/phenogrammar distinction, is based on ideas from type theory and functional programming and comes equipped with a grammar library supporting 30 languages.

1 Introduction

Writing deep linguistic grammars has been considered a highly specialized skill. As the use of statistical methods has increased, new generations of computational linguists are getting less and less prepared for grammar writing tasks. A part of the problem is the steep learning curve in tools: systems like LKB (Copestake, 2002) and XLE (Xerox Linguistic Environment) are designed for professional linguists. Getting started with their use requires substantial training, and installing the tools requires large and unfamiliar software packages, in addition to a firm knowledge of operating system command-line tools.

GF (Ranta, 2004) is a more recent grammar formalism, born so to say in the middle of the statistical era. GF shares the ambition of the "classical" formalisms to enable deep linguistic descriptions, which it wants to support with some new ideas: type theory, functional programming, and an explicit tecto/phenogrammar distinction. However, GF was also meant to be a formalism for "ordinary" programmers without linguistic training. Thus the majority of the currently 30 languages included in the GF Resource Grammar Library (Ranta, 2009a) are in fact written by students and scholars in computer science, who find the GF style of programming familiar from other contexts, in particular compiler construction (Appel, 1998).

However, the GF approach has a "nerdy" flavour to it, in particular requiring coping with command line tools, text editors, and Haskell libraries. Some programmers are helped by the Eclipse plug-in (Camilleri, 2012), but installing both GF and Eclipse on a personal computer can be a daunting task for many.

The present paper describes an attempt to eliminate all trouble with software installation from linguistic grammar writing. We describe a grammar engineering tool that resides in the cloud and can be used in ordinary web browsers. The tool supports writing grammars in the cloud, compiling them to executable parsers and translation systems, and finally running and testing them in the cloud. Thus an entire grammar project can be written and used without installing any specific software. The project can also be published and shared, so that many users can work on the same grammars (although not simultaneously yet in the current version).

The cloud-based GF editor has been used on several tutorial courses and self-studies. It enables absolute beginners to write their first grammar and parse examples in 10 minutes. It scales up to most of the grammars described in the GF book (Ranta, 2011), although it has some limitations, in partic-

Proceedings of the Grammar Engineering Across Frameworks (GEAF) Workshop, 53rd Annual Meeting of the ACL and 7th IJCNLP, pages 41–48,
Beijing, China, July 26-31, 2015. ©2015 Association for Computational Linguistics

```
abstract Foods = {

flags startcat = Comment;

cat Comment; Kind; Item; Quality;

fun Pred : Item -> Quality -> Comment;

    This, That : Kind -> Item;

    Bread, Fish, Wine : Kind;

    Very : Quality -> Quality;
    Bad, Good : Quality;
    Cold, Warm : Quality;
}
```

Figure 1: Abstract syntax `Food.gf`.

```
concrete FoodsGer of Foods =

open SyntaxGer, LexiconGer in {

lincat Comment = Utt;
       Kind = CN;
       Item = NP;
       Quality = AP;

lin
  Pred item qual = mkUtt(mkCl item qual);
  This kind = mkNP this_Det kind;
  That kind = mkNP that_Det kind;
  Bread = mkCN bread_N;
  Fish = mkCN fish_N;
  Wine = mkCN wine_N;
  Very quality = mkAP very_AdA quality;
  Bad = mkAP bad_A;
  Good = mkAP good_A;
  Cold = mkAP cold_A;
  Warm = mkAP warm_A;
}
```

Figure 2: Concrete syntax `FoodGer.gf`.

ular a simplified module system, which makes it unpractical for larger tasks. But students who have got the first experience of grammar writing without the overhead of installation troubles are more likely to proceed to the full-scale systems when they feel the need for it.

1.1 Grammar development with GF

Writing a multilingual grammar in GF consists of writing (1) an abstract syntax that captures the meanings of interest and (2) a number of concrete syntaxes that map the meanings of the abstract syntax to concrete representations in the natural (or formal) languages relevant to the application.

Traditionally, GF grammars are created in a text editor. For example, to create a grammar for comments about food, the grammar author would create an abstract syntax file `Food.gf` (Figure 1) and perhaps a concrete syntax file `FoodsGer.gf` for German (Figure 2). But text editors know very little (if anything) about the syntax of GF grammars, and thus provide little guidance for novice GF users. Instead, to be able to write grammars like the one above, users have to rely on separately available documentation (manuals, tutorials and books) for guidance.

For testing, grammars can be loaded in the GF shell. For example, by loading `FoodsGer.gf`, the user can check that the German sentence *dieses Brot ist sehr gut* can be parsed and represented as `Pred (This Bread) (Very Good)` in the abstract syntax.

GF grammar source files can also be compiled to Portable Grammar Format files (Angelov et al., 2010) that can be used with the GF run-time library to include natural language processing in applications. The key operations provided by the run-time library are parsing, generation, and (by combining the former two) translation. The GF run-time library is also available as a web service, which can be used to create interactive natural language web applications (Bringert et al., 2009; Ranta et al., 2010). Examples can be seen in Figures 6 and 7.

While applications based on GF grammars could be made available online by using the GF web service, until now the grammars themselves had to be created with offline tools that the grammar developer had to download and install on his/her own computer. With the cloud-based editor presented here, the grammars can also be created online.

1.2 Outline

In section 2 we describe the cloud-based grammar editor introduced above. In section 3 we describe a new technique for *example-based grammar writing* that we are adding support for in the cloud-based editor. This makes it possible for a user with minimal knowledge of GF grammar construction to add new languages to a multilingual grammar by translating automatically generated examples in one of the existing languages to the new language. In section 4 we present some implementation details and in sections 5 and 6 we describe related and future work.

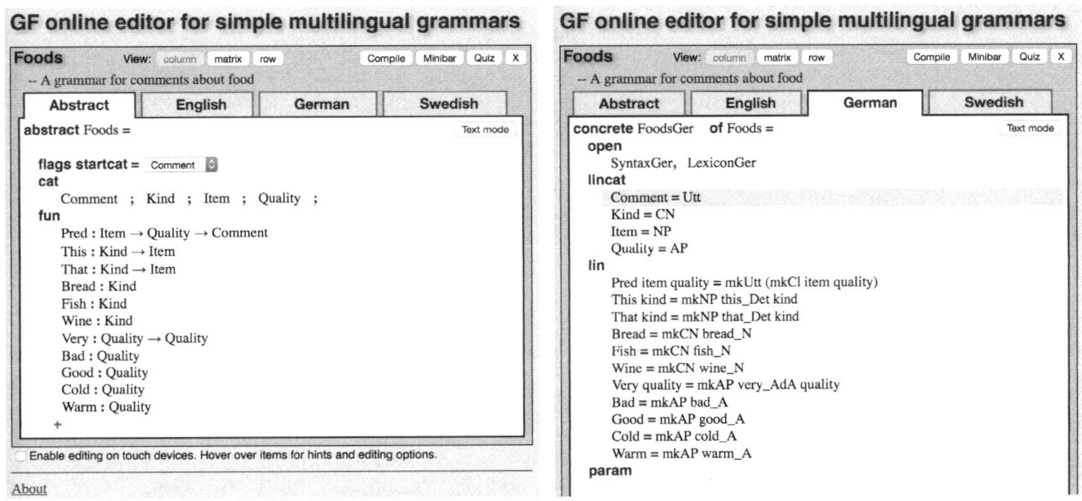

Figure 3: GF online editor for simple multilingual grammars

2 The GF online grammar editor

As the name suggests, the *GF online editor for simple multilingual grammars* is available online (Hallgren, 2013), so all that is needed to use the editor is a device with a reasonably modern web browser. Even smartphones and tablets can be used. To help novice grammar authors, the editor provides some guidance, e.g. by showing a skeleton grammar file and hinting how the parts should be filled in. When a new part is added to the grammar, it is immediately checked for errors.

Figure 3 illustrates what the editor looks like. Editing operations are accessed by clicking on editing symbols embedded in the grammar display: **+**, **x** and **%** to add, delete and edit items. These are revealed when hovering over items. On touch devices, hovering is in some cases simulated by tapping, but there is also a button to "Enable editing on touch devices" that reveals all editing symbols.

The current version of the editor supports a small but useful subset of the GF grammar notation. Grammars consist of one module for the abstract syntax, and a number of modules for concrete syntaxes. Proper error checking is done on the fly for abstract syntax, but not (yet) for concrete syntax.

Grammars can import modules from the *Resource Grammar Library* (Ranta, 2009a), freeing the grammar author from dealing directly with the linguistic complexities of natural languages, such as inflection and agreement.

2.1 Abstract syntax

The definition of an abstract syntax consists of

- a list of inherited abstract syntaxes,
- a list of *category names*, C_1 ; ... ; C_n,
- a list of *functions*, $Fun_i : C_{i_1} \to \ldots \to C_{i_n}$
- and the designation of a *start category*.

This is somewhat restricted compared to the full GF grammar formalism, e.g. dependent types are not supported.

Available editing operations include:

- Inherited abstract syntaxes can be added and removed.
- Categories can be added, removed and renamed. When renaming a category, occurrences of it in function types will be updated accordingly.
- Functions can be added, removed, renamed and edited. Concrete syntaxes are updated to reflect changes.
- Functions can be reordered using drag-and-drop.

The editor checks the abstract syntax for correctness as it is entered. Syntactically incorrect function definitions are rejected. Semantic errors such as duplicated definitions or references to undefined categories, are highlighted. This is enough to ensure that a grammar that is accepted by the editor will also be accepted by the GF grammar compiler.

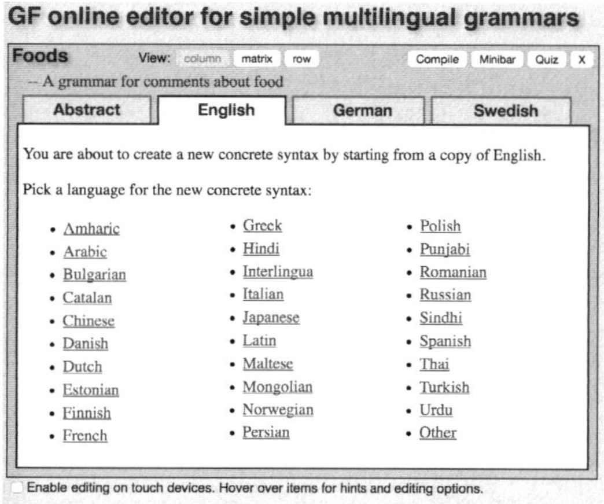

Figure 4: Adding a new concrete syntax

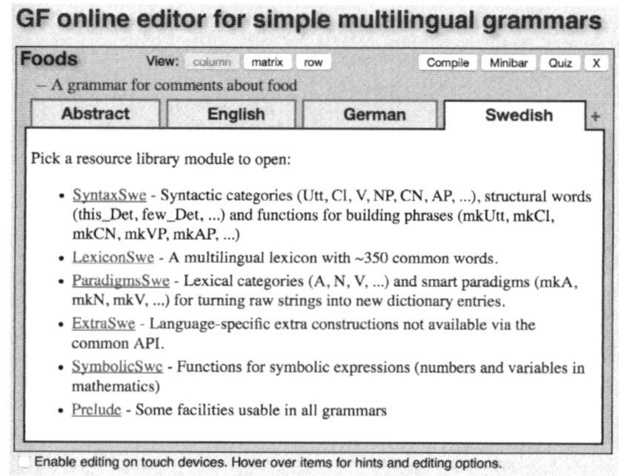

Figure 5: Opening modules from the Resource Grammar Library

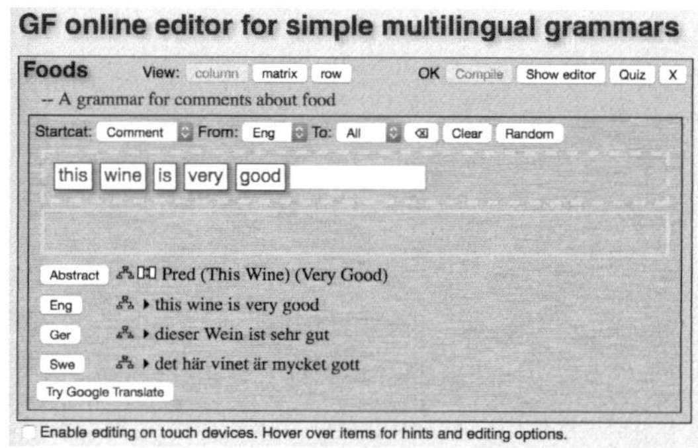

Figure 6: Testing grammars in the Minibar

2.2 Concrete syntax

When adding a new concrete syntax to a grammar, the editor shows a list of supported natural languages and the user just picks one. See Figure 4. The name of the new module is filled in automatically based on naming conventions, e.g. `FoodsEng` if abstract syntax is called `Foods` and we are adding a translation to English. The body of the new concrete syntax can be created by copying and modifying an existing concrete syntax, or by starting with a skeleton based on the abstract syntax.

The key components of a concrete syntax are *linearization types* for the categories and *linearizations* for the functions in the abstract syntax. The editor automatically provides correct left-hand sides for these, since they are determined by the abstract syntax, while the right-hand sides can be edited freely.

The editor allows a concrete syntax to open some of the relevant Resource Grammar Library modules. A list of suitable library modules is shown, e.g., `SyntaxEng` and `LexiconEng` in a concrete syntax for English, so the user does not need to know their names by heart. See Figure 5.

The editor also supports definitions of *parameter types* and auxiliary *operations*, but usually it is enough to rely on the types and operations provided by the Resource Grammar Library.

The editor checks all user editable parts of the concrete syntax for syntactic correctness as they are entered. Duplicated definitions of parameter types or operations are highlighted. Checks for other semantic errors are delayed until the grammar is compiled.

2.3 Compiling and testing grammars

When pressing the *Compile* button, the grammar is uploaded to the server and compiled with GF, and any errors not detected by the editor will be reported. Error-free grammars can be tested by clicking on the the *Minibar* button, which is a web-based translation tool, and the *Quiz* button, which is a web-based language training tool (Abolahrar, 2011). See Figures 6 and 7.

2.4 Grammars in the cloud

While grammars created in the editor are stored locally in the device by the browser, it is also possible to store grammars in the cloud. Each device is initially assigned to its own unique cloud and has its own set of grammars, but it is also possible to merge clouds and share a common set of grammars between multiple devices.

Users can also choose to "publish" a grammar. A copy of the grammar is then added to a list of

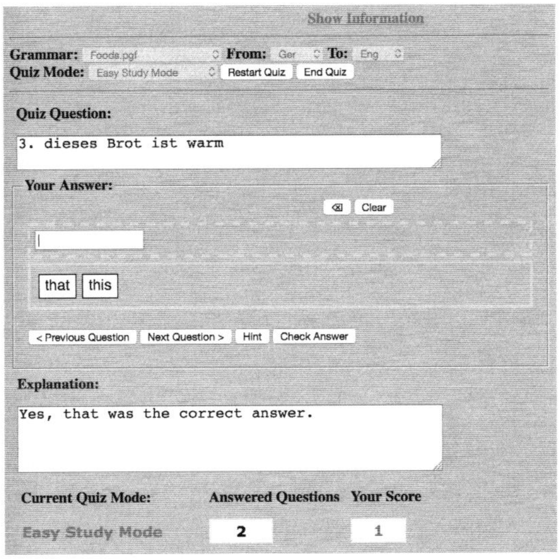

Figure 7: Testing grammars in the Translation Quiz

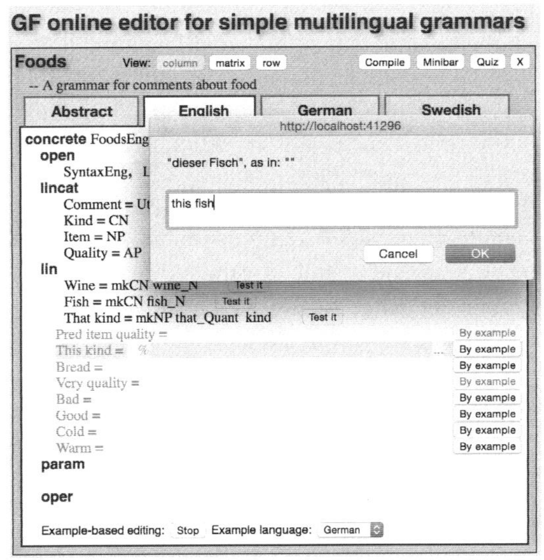

Figure 8: Example-based grammar construction

grammars visible to all users of the cloud-based grammar editor.

3 Example-based grammar writing

The example-based grammar writing mechanism is aimed at helping users who build concrete grammars using the resource grammar for the given language. The resource library provides over 300 functions for building grammatical constructs such as predication, complementation, etc (Ranta, 2009b). Using the resource library is advantageous on one hand, because it alleviates the difficulty of reimplementing language-specific features every time when writing a grammar for the language, but on the other hand it assumes a working knowledge of the resource library, which could lead to a larger overall effort. We aim at freeing users from this burden by making it possible for them to write function linearizations by giving example of their usage. In the current scenario, we assume that a large lexicon covering the words that could be used in the grammar is available already. We will use the resource grammar enhanced with the larger dictionary for parsing the examples from the user in order to infer the right linearization form.

Since the functions from the grammar could take arguments, in order to give an example for the usage of a certain function, we need to have one example for each of its arguments in order to get more precise information about the behavior of the function. For this reason, only the function for which all arguments can be found among the already implemented functions, are highlighted as available for the example-based method.

In order to clarify the usage of a certain function, its context is made explicit by embedding the function into a tree returning the start category, like in Figure 8 where "this fish" is used to make phrases like "this fish is delicious". Since certain parts of the phrase are not relevant for the task, they are underspecified by using "?" instead. In case that the grammar returns more than one parse tree, the results are ranked in the descending order of their probability (defined in the corresponding resource grammar or defined by the user), and the first tree from which the arguments can be abstracted is chosen as the linearization tree.

The technique has been used as an experimental way for developing a tourist phrasebook grammar in GF for 4 languages (Ranta et al., 2011), but no tool support was available at that time. The positive results obtained were a strong motivation to make the method available to end users as part of a GF grammar writing system.

The example-based grammar writing system is still work in progress and the basic prototype currently available will be further developed and improved. It is possible to use it already for 5 languages where a large dictionary is available in GF (English, Swedish, Finnish, Bulgarian, French).

4 Implementation

The implementation of the cloud-based editor consists of a client-side part and a server-side part.

The client-side part is written directly in JavaScript. In total, roughly 6350 lines of JavaScript (180KB) is loaded by the browser when opening the editor. This divides roughly into 2800 lines written specifically for the editor, 2600 lines of code for other components (the minibar) and 750 lines of supporting library code.

All server-side code is written in Haskell. This includes the GF grammar compiler, the PGF runtime library and the PGF web service (Bringert et al., 2009). We created a new GF cloud service API (Hallgren, 2014) to support the editor. It includes functionality for grammar syntax checking, grammar upload, grammar compilation and access to the GF shell. It's implemented as 500 lines of Haskell code.

To support example-based grammar writing, we added 200 lines of client-side JavaScript code and 680 lines of Haskell code in the server.

5 Related work

GF is a grammar formalism comparable in expressive power to HPSG (Pollard and Sag, 1994) and LFG (Bresnan, 1982), but different due to the distinction between the abstract and concrete dimension of a grammar, along with the possibility to share the abstract syntax which makes translation between any pair of languages possible. In the same way, the GF resource library could be compared to two other multilingual resources based on the above-mentioned formalisms: LinGO Grammar Matrix (Bender et al., 2002) for HPSG and ParGram (Butt et al., 2002) for LFG.

Since the task of developing a multilingual grammar within such a grammar formalism poses specific challenges, each system comes equipped with its own IDE/editor that aids the grammar development process. LinGO Grammar Matrix has a grammar-customization system (Bender et al., 2010) and ParGram has XLFG, a customized IDE (Clément, 2009). While XLFG allows storing and editing grammars, it is only available for English and French. The customization system from LinGO Grammar Matrix allows specifying linguistic features of certain grammar constructions in the shape of a questionnaire and it is mainly used for developing new language resources for the Matrix library. The further use of the resources is supported by a parser, sentence generator and facilities for profiling and regression testing (Oepen and Flickinger, 1998).

In addition to the cloud-based IDE, GF also has a desktop IDE, implemented as an Eclipse plugin (Camilleri, 2012).

6 Future work

The GF grammar editor described here already supports a useful subset of the GF grammar notation. Some of the guidance and error checking is done in the editor on the client side (resulting in well integrated user friendly error indications), some is delegated to the server (resulting in less user friendly error messages). We do not expect to create a full implementation of GF that runs in the web browser.

If we want to support the full-fledged GF grammar formalism, the easy way out would be to duplicate a typical desktop development environment in the browser, i.e. create an environment with a text editor and command line tools, or perhaps a more integrated Eclipse-like environment. But we would prefer to create something that is more interactive and provides more guidance for novice users, so we are thinking of an interactive development environment in the style of proof assistants based on type theory, such as Alfa (Hallgren, 2004) and Agda (Norell, 2007). However, being a batch compiler, GF does currently not provide an API that makes it easy to create this kind of development environment. If a GF server with an appropriate API becomes available, it should be possible to extend the editor to support a larger fragment of GF, to provide more user guidance, more user friendly error reporting, and in general make more of the functionality in the existing GF tools accessible directly from the online editor.

More work is needed on the grammar cloud storage service. In particular, it is currently not suitable for multiple users developing a grammar in collaboration. This could be done by interfacing with a online collaboration tool (like GitHub), or by allowing concurrent access to shared grammars and propagating edits to all users in real-time (like in Google Docs).

Combining the cloud-based grammar editor with other cloud-based tools opens up possibilities for new applications, such as a tourist phrasebook that can be extended by the user with a new topic of interest, or a language training tool (like the one in Figure 7) that instructors or students can customize for training or testing a particular vocabulary or particular grammatical forms. It should be possible to make this kind of customizations in minutes, without installing any software.

Future work on the example-based method includes combining it with traditional grammar writing and the possibility to develop more languages in parallel and use one as an example for the other. Moreover, since currently the method works for the case when the linearization type is a category from the resource library (noun phrase, sentence, etc.), one could also extend the algorithm in order to handle record types comprising more such syntactic categories. Last but not least, we aim at covering languages for which large dictionaries are not available by making the method robust to unknown words that could be later implemented by the user.

References

Elnaz Abolahrar. 2011. Multilingual Grammar-Based Language Training: Computational Methods and Tools. Master's thesis, Chalmers University of Technology.

Krasimir Angelov, Björn Bringert, and Aarne Ranta. 2010. PGF: A Portable Run-time Format for Type-theoretical Grammars. *Journal of Logic, Language and Information*, 19:201–228. 10.1007/s10849-009-9112-y.

Andrew W. Appel. 1998. *Modern Compiler Implementation in ML*. Cambridge University Press.

Emily M. Bender, Dan Flickinger, and Stephan Oepen. 2002. The grammar matrix: an open-source starter-kit for the rapid development of cross-linguistically consistent broad-coverage precision grammars. In *COLING-02 on Grammar engineering and evaluation*, pages 1–7, Morristown, NJ, USA. Association for Computational Linguistics.

Emily M. Bender, Scott Drellishak, Antske Fokkens, Laurie Poulson, and Safiyyah Saleem. 2010. Grammar Customization. *Research on Language & Computation*, 8(1):23–72. 10.1007/s11168-010-9070-1.

Joan Bresnan. 1982. *The Mental Representation of Grammatical Relations*. MIT Press.

Björn Bringert, Krasimir Angelov, and Aarne Ranta. 2009. Grammatical framework web service. In *Proceedings of the Demonstrations Session at EACL 2009*, pages 9–12, Athens, Greece, April. Association for Computational Linguistics.

Miriam Butt, Helge Dyvik, Tracy Holloway King, Hiroshi Masuichi, and Christian Rohrer. 2002. The Parallel Grammar project. In *COLING-02 on Grammar engineering and evaluation*, pages 1–7, Morristown, NJ, USA. Association for Computational Linguistics.

John J. Camilleri. 2012. An IDE for the Grammatical Framework. Gothenburg, Sweden, June.

Lionel Clément. 2009. XLFG5 Documentation. `https://signes.bordeaux.inria.fr/xlfg5/doc/en/`, October.

Ann Copestake. 2002. *Implementing typed feature structure grammars*, volume 110. CSLI publications Stanford.

Thomas Hallgren. 2004. Home Page of the Proof Editor Alfa. `www.cse.chalmers.se/~hallgren/Alfa/`.

Thomas Hallgren. 2013. GF online editor for simple multilingual grammars. `http://cloud.grammaticalframework.org/gfse/`.

Thomas Hallgren. 2014. GF Cloud Service API. `http://cloud.grammaticalframework.org/gf-cloud-api.html`.

Ulf Norell. 2007. *Towards a practical programming language based on dependent type theory*. Ph.D. thesis, Department of Computer Science and Engineering, Chalmers University of Technology, SE-412 96 Göteborg, Sweden, September.

Stephan Oepen and Daniel P. Flickinger. 1998. Towards Systematic Grammar Profiling Test Suite Technology Ten Years After. *Special Issue on Evaluation), 411*, 12:411–436.

Carl Pollard and Ivan A. Sag. 1994. *Head-Driven Phrase Structure Grammar*. University of Chicago Press.

Aarne Ranta, Krasimir Angelov, and Thomas Hallgren. 2010. Tools for multilingual grammar-based translation on the web. In *Proceedings of the ACL 2010 System Demonstrations*, pages 66–71, Uppsala, Sweden, July. Association for Computational Linguistics.

Aarne Ranta, Ramona Enache, and Grégoire Détrez. 2011. Controlled Language for Everyday Use: the MOLTO Phrasebook. *Proceeding of the 2nd Workshop on Controlled Natural Languages (CNL 2010)*.

Aarne Ranta. 2004. Grammatical Framework: A Type-Theoretical Grammar Formalism. *The Journal of Functional Programming*, 14(2):145–189.

Aarne Ranta. 2009a. The GF resource grammar library. *Linguistic Issues in Language Technology*, 2(2).

Aarne Ranta. 2009b. Grammars as Software Libraries. In Yves Bertot, Gérard Huet, Jean-Jacques. Lévy, and Gordon Plotkin, editors, *From Semantics to Computer Science. Essays in Honour of*

Gilles Kahn, pages 281–308. Cambridge University Press. `http://www.cse.chalmers.se/~aarne/articles/libraries-kahn.pdf`.

Aarne Ranta. 2011. *Grammatical Framework: Programming with Multilingual Grammars*. CSLI Publications, Stanford. ISBN-10: 1-57586-626-9 (Paper), 1-57586-627-7 (Cloth).

Formalising the Swedish Constructicon in Grammatical Framework

Normunds Gruzitis[1] **Dana Dannélls**[2] **Benjamin Lyngfelt**[2] **Aarne Ranta**[1]
[1]Department of Computer Science and Engineering
[2]Department of Swedish
University of Gothenburg
[1]{name.surname}@cse.gu.se, [2]{name.surname}@svenska.gu.se

Abstract

This paper presents a semi-automatic approach to acquire a computational construction grammar from the semi-formal Swedish Constructicon. The implementation is based on the resource grammar library provided by Grammatical Framework and can be seen as an extension to the existing Swedish resource grammar. An important consequence of this work is that it generates feedback, explicit and implicit, on how to improve the annotation consistency and adequacy of the original construction resource.

1 Introduction

Constructicon is a collection of conventionalized pairings of form and meaning (or function), typically based on principles of Construction Grammar (Goldberg, 2013).

The formalisation and implementation of a wide coverage construction grammar is a highly relevant task. From the linguistic point of view, it leads to new insights on the interaction between the lexicon and the grammar, as well as it allows for testing the linguistic descriptions of constructions. From the language technology point of view, the account of constructions facilitates language processing in both monolingual and multilingual settings, e.g. in information extraction and machine translation.

Several approaches to Construction Grammar have been proposed. Remarkable examples include Sign-Based Construction Grammar (Boas and Sag, 2012) that uses Head-Driven Phrase Structure Grammar (Pollard and Sag, 1994) as the underlying formalism, Fluid Construction Grammar (Steels, 2013) and Embodied Construction Grammar (Bergen and Chang, 2013).

While the previous work has been mainly focused on English, our work is currently focused on Swedish. However, the main difference is that we test Grammatical Framework, GF (Ranta, 2004), as a formalism and a toolkit for implementing computational construction grammars. GF provides a built-in support for multilingual grammars, which has a great potential for implementing, unifying and interlinking constructions of different languages, which, in turn, would be particularly beneficial for the use in machine translation and second-language learning.

In this paper we describe a methodology on how to systematically formalise the semi-formal representation of the Swedish Constructicon in GF, showing that a GF construction grammar can be, to a large extent, acquired automatically. A side result of our work is that it has also helps to improve the original construction resource.

2 Background

2.1 Swedish Constructicon (SweCcn)

SweCcn[1] is a comparatively large open database of Swedish constructions – partially schematic multi-word units having both fixed and variable parts (Lyngfelt et al., 2012). It particularly addresses constructions of relevance for second-language learning, but also covers argument structure constructions, which concern matters of transitivity, voice, and event structure. Construction descriptions are manually derived from corpus examples, and some of the examples are manually annotated and added to each SweCcn entry. A simplified example of how a construction is described in SweCcn is given in Table 1.

Construction elements (CE) are either internal or external. The internal CEs are a part of the construction while the external CEs are a part of the valency of the construction. In the structure sketches, the internal CEs are bounded by brackets. CEs are described in more detail by attribute-

[1]http://spraakbanken.gu.se/eng/sweccn

Proceedings of the Grammar Engineering Across Frameworks (GEAF) Workshop, 53rd Annual Meeting of the ACL and 7th IJCNLP, pages 49–56,
Beijing, China, July 26-31, 2015. ©2015 Association for Computational Linguistics

Name	REFLEXIV_RESULTATIV
Category	VP
Frame	CAUSATION
Defintion	[Someone/something]$_{NP}$ performs/undergoes [an action]$_{Activity}$ that leads (or is supposed to lead) the [actor/theme]$_{Pn}$, expressed by reflexive, to [a state]$_{Result}$.
Structure	`NP [V Pn`$_{refl}$ `AP]`
Internal	Activity: {`cat=V, role=Activity`} Pn: {`cat=Pn`$_{refl}$`, role=Actor|Theme`} Result: {`cat=AP, role=Result`}
External	NP: {`cat=NP, role=Actor|Theme`}
Example	*Peter*$_{NP}$ [*äter*$_{Activity}$ *sig*$_{Pn}$ *mätt*$_{Result}$]

Table 1: A simplified description of the Swedish construction REFLEXIV_RESULTATIV. The example literally translates as 'Peter eats himself full'.

value matrices that specify their syntactic and semantic features.

Fixed CEs are represented by lexical units (LU), and they refer to entries in SALDO, the Swedish Associative Thesaurus (Borin et al., 2013), which is the core lexicon of a large macro-resource for Swedish, developed within the Swedish FrameNet++ project (Borin et al., 2010).

Many constructions have a referential meaning, more specifically, they are frame-bearing and are thus linked to FrameNet frames. There is also an ongoing work to link, when possible, the SweCcn constructions with constructions in Berkeley Constructicon (Bäckström et al., 2014) as well as other constructicons, notably the one for Brazilian Portuguese (Torrent et al., 2014).

It should be noted that a central part of construction descriptions in SweCcn is the free text definitions. For example, the construction REFLEXIV_RESULTATIV roughly means 'become AP by V-ing'. Hence, *äta sig mätt* 'eat himself full' and *skrika sig hes* 'shouting himself hoarse' are instances of the construction, whereas *känna sig trött* 'feel himself tired' and *skratta sig lycklig* 'laugh himself lucky' are not. The difference is captured by the free text definition, but not by the formal features, therefore it unfortunately gets lost in the automatic translation to GF.

In this experiment, we use a recent version of SweCcn (a snapshot taken on June 9, 2015) which contains 374 entries describing constructions of different grammatical categories such as VP, NP and S (see Table 2).

Category	Total	Ratio	FrameNet
VP	105	28%	77
NP	85	23%	54
S	77	21%	50
PP	26	7%	22
AdvP	23	6%	19
XP	16	4%	4
AP	14	4%	13
other	28	7%	19

Table 2: The number of constructions in SweCcn. The category XP represents any phrase type. The column FrameNet shows the number of constructions linked to the Swedish FrameNet.

2.2 Grammatical Framework (GF)

GF (Ranta, 2004) is a grammar formalism characterized by its two-level approach to natural language representation. One level, the abstract syntax, accounts for the language-independent aspects, and the other level, the concrete syntax, accounts for the language-specific aspects. The same abstract syntax can be equipped with many concrete syntaxes – reversible mappings from abstract syntax trees to records (feature structures) and strings – making the grammar multilingual.

Most importantly, GF provides a general-purpose resource grammar library, RGL (Ranta, 2009), for currently 30 languages, all implementing the same abstract syntax.

In order to hide the low-level details, RGL has a high-level interface that provides constructors like `mkCl : NP -> VP -> Cl` for building a clause from a NP and a VP.[2] The resource grammars take care of agreement and word order.

One of the most developed languages in RGL, in terms of syntactic and lexical coverage, is Swedish. Its resource grammar also includes over 100,000 lexical entries from SALDO.[3]

3 Preprocessing of SweCcn

In the current experiment, we consider only the 105 constructions of type VP (verb phrase) from which we exclude 9 whose status is 'suggestion'. Descriptions of the suggested constructions are too immature to be processed. Currently we also

[2] http://www.grammaticalframework.org/lib/doc/synopsis.html

[3] http://www.grammaticalframework.org/lib/src/swedish/DictSwe.gf

do not include the 16 XP constructions which are relevant to any phrase type, including VP.

We have chosen to begin with VP constructions because they are dominating in SweCcn, and they have the most complex internal structure – if our approach can handle these constructions then it should also be applicable for the rest.

According to the SweCcn annotation manual,[4] constructions are described at two levels of detail:

1. A flat structure sketch that lists the formal elements in the construction (see *Structure* in Table 1). Each CE is represented in terms of grammatical category (either word class or phrase type), LU or just word form. The list of CEs follows the expected word order. A structure sketch may specify alternative realisation patterns of the same construction.

2. A set of feature matrices, one per CE (see *Internal* and *External* in Table 1), that specify additional morphosyntactic constraints which may be omitted in the more general sketch for the sake of simplicity to a human reader. Additionally, the feature matrices often specify the semantic roles and grammatical functions, but we do not take this information into account in the current work.
   The word order is encoded only by the structure sketches; it is not reflected by the corresponding feature matrices as they can be potentially reused by alternative patterns of the same construction. Because the linking between the sketches and matrices is not explicit, and the implicit links (matching categories, LUs etc.) are not unique in general, the automatic mapping can be ambiguous. In practice, however, it happens rarely.

Constructions may have optional CEs, alternative types of CEs or alternative LUs, and even alternative word order. In the structure sketches, optional CEs are delimited by parentheses, and alternative types/LUs are separated by a bar:

[V av^1 Pn$_{refl}$ (NP)]

[behöva^1 NP$_1$ till^1 NP$_2$|VP]

[snacka^1|prata^1|tala^1 NP$_{indef}$]

[N|Adj+städa^1]

[4] https://svn.spraakdata.gu.se/sb/fnplusplus/pub/constructicon/manual/sweccnmanual.pdf

Note that the variable CEs (represented by grammatical categories) may have indices denoting difference, formal identity (repetition), coreference, etc. In the case of a lexical construction that represents a compound word, its internal CEs are delimited by the plus sign indicating the concatenation. Suffixation is indicated by the hyphen.

The automatic preprocessing of SweCcn entries consists of four steps:

1. Normalization of the structure sketches and attribute values in the feature matrices. SweCcn entries have been annotated manually, therefore inconsistently used spaces, inconsistently used delimiters of alternative CE types as well as inconsistent representation of auxiliary or function CEs (e.g. *sig*^{1} vs. *Pn*$_{refl}$ vs. *refl*) is common.

2. In case of optional CEs and alternative types of CEs, there are formally several constructions compressed in one. The original structures are rewritten so that for each combination there is a separate alternative structure. For instance, [V av^1 Pn$_{refl}$ (NP)] is rewritten to [V av^1 Pn$_{refl}$ NP] | [V av^1 Pn$_{refl}$].
   This however does not apply to alternative LUs. If a CE is represented by a fixed set of LUs, we assume that they are interchangeable (synonymous). Otherwise they should be either split into alternative constructions (separate entries), or the CE should be made more general.[5]

3. The rewritten structure sketches are enriched with additional morphosyntactic information from the feature matrices, so that a complete description is at hand. The mapping of CEs between the two layers of annotation is based on values of the grammatical category and LU attributes in the feature matrices (see Table 1). Although such mapping in general is based on a partial comparison as well as it can be ambiguous, it has not led to incorrect results in the selected dataset,[6] because we do not consider the semantic roles.

[5] If a list of non-interchangeable but frame-evoking LUs is replaced by a general grammatical category, the set of possible target words is still implicitly restricted by the FrameNet frame which is evoked by the whole construction.

[6] Provided that the specifications are consistent across the two layers.

4. The grammatical categories used in SweCcn are converted to GF RGL categories. In specific cases, the conversion may lead into a more general or more specific description as well as it may include the morphosyntactic tags and may depend on CEs in the context. For instance, categories Adv, AdvP and PP are all generalized to Adv while the specification NP_{indef} is elaborated in three alternative substructures: `[aSg_Det CN] | [aPl_Det CN] | CN`, where *aSg_Det* is a function representing the indefinite article and requiring the singular agreement, *aPl_Det* requires the plural agreement, and CN is a category that represents common nouns (including modifiers, except determiners). This requires a subsequent rewriting of the whole construction as described in Step 2. Few categories are not converted at this step; their conversion is postponed to the generation of the GF grammar. For instance, Pc (participle) and PcP (participle phrase) are not converted to V and VP respectively, as they have to be treated differently in the concrete syntax: PcP is a VP that is further converted to AP or Adv as illustrated by FÅ_RESULTATIV.AGENTIV in Sections 4.1 and 4.2.

Out of the 96 VP constructions that were processed, only 43 turned out to be consistent in the first attempt. For more than a half of constructions, various inconsistencies were detected and reported to SweCcn developers for manual inspection and correction. After several iterations, the number of consistent VP constructions increased to 93. The remaining 3 are different corner cases that are actually consistent but are not yet supported by the preprocessor and are thus skipped.

The following is a list of representative VP constructions with their original and rewritten structure descriptions that we use in Section 4 to illustrate the automatic generation of the GF grammar:

BEHÖVA_NÅGOT_TILL_NÅGOT:
behöva mat till festen 'need food to the party'
behöva^1 NP$_1$ till^1 NP$_2$|VP →
behöva$_V$ NP$_1$ till$_{Prep}$ NP$_2$
| behöva$_V$ NP till$_{Prep}$ VP

FÅ_RESULTATIV.AGENTIV:
få gräsmattan klippt 'get the lawn trimmed'
få^0 NP PcP → få$_V$ NP PcP$_{perf}$

GÖRA_SIG_ADVP:
gör sig bra 'does himself well'
göra^1 Pn$_{refl}$ AdvP → göra$_V$ refl$_{Pron}$ Adv

SNACKA_NP:
prata skolminnen 'talk school memories'
snacka^1|prata^1|tala^1 NP$_{indef}$ →
snacka|prata|tala$_V$ aSg_Det CN
| snacka|prata|tala$_V$ aPl_Det CN
| snacka|prata|tala$_V$ CN

VERBA_AV_SIG.TRANSITIV:
ta av mig skorna 'take off myself shoes'
V av^1 Pn$_{refl}$ (NP) →
V av$_{Prep}$ refl$_{Pron}$ NP | V av$_{Prep}$ refl$_{Pron}$

X-STÄDA:
storstäda 'bigclean'
N|Adj+städa^1 → N + städa$_V$ | A + städa$_V$

Note that we ignore the SALDO sense identifiers. We ignore the external CEs in the current approach as well, as they should be attached to constructions by the general syntactic rules already provided by GF RGL. It is satisfactory also from the future translation point of view, as the translation of external CEs should be compositional.

4 Generation of a GF Grammar

The rewritten structural descriptions of constructions, as described in Section 3, provide sufficient information to generate both the abstract and the concrete syntax of a SweCcn-based construction grammar, an extension to the Swedish GF resource grammar.[7]

4.1 Abstract Syntax

The generation of the abstract syntax is rather straight forward. Each construction is represented by one or more functions depending on how many alternative structure descriptions are produced in the preprocessing steps. The name of a function corresponds to the name of the construction suffixed by an index if there is more than one function per construction. For the current input data, the 93 VP constructions resulted in 127 functions. The maximum and average numbers are respectively 6 and 1.4 functions per construction.[8]

[7] https://github.com/GrammaticalFramework/gf-contrib/tree/master/SweCcn

[8] The max number is produced by SNACKA_NP.EMFAS: [snacka^1|prata^1 (AP) NP$_{indef}$].

Each function takes one or more arguments that correspond to the variable CEs of the respective alternative construction description. In the rewritten structure descriptions, the variable CEs can be formally distinguished from fixed CEs (LUs and structural words) by the first letter of each CE: the variable CEs always start with an upper case letter while the fixed CEs start with a lower case letter. The fixed CEs are not represented by the abstract syntax. The variable CEs are represented only by their grammatical categories; other morphosyntactic constraints (if any) are handled by the concrete syntax.

Constructions listed at the end of Section 3 are represented by the following abstract functions:

```
behöva_något_till_något1: NP -> NP -> VP
behöva_något_till_något2: NP -> VP -> VP

få_resultativ_agentiv: NP -> VP -> VP

göra_sig_AdvP: Adv -> VP

snacka_NP1: CN -> VP
snacka_NP2: CN -> VP
snacka_NP3: CN -> VP

verba_av_sig_transitiv1: V -> NP -> VP
verba_av_sig_transitiv2: V -> VP

x_städa1: N -> VP
x_städa2: A -> VP
```

4.2 Concrete Syntax

As our initial investigation unveiled, many constructions can be implemented in GF by systematically applying the high-level RGL constructors. For instance, behöva_något_till_något$_1$ can be implemented as shown in Figure 1 by first making a two-place verb (V2) from the V element and then combining it with the first NP element into a VP. The preposition can be combined with the second NP element into a prepositional phrase (Adv) which can then be attached to the VP. The question is how to make such constructor applications systematically given the various construction descriptions.

Essentially, this is a parsing problem itself. We can look at CEs as words in the construction description language for which we need a grammar to combine the lists of CEs into trees of RGL constructors and their arguments.

In order to address this issue, we have defined an auxiliary GF grammar to generate the implementation of functions in the GF construction grammar. To keep the code-generating grammar simple, it accepts only the categories of CEs, some additional constraints and certain structural words. The preprocessed construction descriptions are generalized before parsing; LUs are inserted back in a post-processing step. For instance, behöva$_V$ NP$_1$ till$_{Prep}$ NP$_2$ is generalised to {V} NP {Prep} NP, where the curly brackets indicate fixed CEs. Fragments of the code-generating grammar related to this structure are listed in Figure 2 and Figure 3.

```
behöva_något_till_något1 np1 np2 =
  mkVP
    (mkVP (mkV2 (mkV "behöver")) np1)
    (mkAdv (mkPrep "till") np2)
```

Figure 1: The expected implementation for the function behöva_något_till_något$_1$.

```
fun mkV2: V -> V2
fun mkVP__V2_NP: V2 -> NP -> VP
fun mkVP__VP_Adv: VP -> Adv -> VP
fun mkAdv: Prep -> NP -> Adv
fun _mkV_: V
fun _mkPrep_: Prep
fun _NP_: NP
```

Figure 2: A simplified fragment of the abstract syntax of the auxiliary code-generating grammar.

According to the auxiliary grammar, the parse tree for "{V} NP {Prep} NP" is

```
mkVP__VP_Adv
  (mkVP__V2_NP (mkV2 _mkV_) _NP_)
  (mkAdv _mkPrep_ _NP_)
```

which corresponds to the expected implementation as shown in Figure 1 after the post-processing is done. The post-processing involves three steps:

1. Remove all suffixes delimited by the double underscore. The suffixes are used just to make the function names unique in the auxiliary grammar.

2. Sequentially replace all placeholders of the fixed CEs, annotated as *_mkX_*, by the actual lexical constructors. In case of verbs, constructors (inflectional paradigms) specified in

```
param Voice = Act | Pass

lincat
  V, V2 = Voice => Str
  VP, NP, Adv, Prep = Str

lin
  mkV2 v = \\voice => v ! voice

  mkVP__V2_NP v2 np = v2 ! Act ++ np
  mkVP__VP_Adv vp adv = vp ++ adv

  mkAdv prep np = prep ++ np

  _mkV_ = table {
    Act => "{V}"
    Pass => "{V_pass}"
  }

  _mkPrep_ = "{Prep}"

  _NP_ = "NP"
```

Figure 3: A simplified fragment of the concrete syntax of the auxiliary code-generating grammar.

the GF implementation of SALDO (see Section 2.2) are reused.

3. Sequentially replace all placeholders of the variable CEs, annotated as *_X_*, by the actual variable names, e.g. replace the first *_NP_* by np_1 and the second *_NP_* by np_2.

Note that the auxiliary code-generating grammar, in general, is ambiguous – it can return several alternative code skeletons for a given CE list. However, it should hold that all alternatives accept and linearise the same strings. Our heuristics is to take the shortest implementation, which is supported by the intuition that the shortest ones correlate with the simplest ones.

If we consider the alternative realization of BEHÖVA_NÅGOT_TILL_NÅGOT represented by the function `behöva_något_till_något₂`, the parsing with the auxiliary grammar fails at the element *VP*. Indeed, there is no straightforward constructor provided by RGL that would combine a Prep with a VP or an Adv (as the *in-order-to*-VP should be first converted to Adv). Thus, a lower level means have to be applied to implement this function.

The implementation generated for the rest of functions listed in Section 4.1 is given below (in a slightly simplified form):

```
få_resultativ_agentiv np vp = mkVP
  (mkV2A (mkV "få"))
  np (PresPartAP vp)

göra_sig_AdvP adv = mkVP
  (mkVP (reflV (mkV "göra"))) adv

snacka_NP1 cn = mkVP
  (mkV2 (mkV ("snacka"|"prata"|..)))
  (mkNP aSg_Det cn)

snacka_NP2 cn = mkVP
  (mkV2 (mkV ("snacka"|"prata"|..)))
  (mkNP aPl_Det cn)

snacka_NP3 cn = mkVP
  (mkV2 (mkV ("snacka"|"prata"|..)))
  (mkNP cn)

verba_av_sig_transitiv1 v np = mkVP
  (mkV2 (reflV
    (partV v (toStr (mkPrep "av")))))
  np

verba_av_sig_transitiv2 v = mkVP
  (reflV
    (partV v (toStr (mkPrep "av"))))

x_städa1 n = mkVP
  (prefixV (toStr n) (mkV "städar"))

x_städa2 a = mkVP
  (prefixV (toStr a) (mkV "städar"))
```

As it was already mentioned, for some functions the implementation has to be based not only on the high-level language-independent interface of RGL but also on low-level language-specific parameters. To keep the GF code generation flexible and functional, we have defined some helper functions (in the construction grammar) that wrap the low-level code and make it reusable. For instance, the helper function *toStr* takes a preposition, adjective or noun and returns its base form as a plain string which can then be passed, for instance, to the RGL function *partV* to make a particle verb, or to another helper function *prefixV* to make a compound verb.

As for LUs, note that they are implemented, in general, as free alternatives, which means that any of them will be accepted while parsing but the first one will always be used for the linearisation.

In the result, given the 127 functions in the abstract syntax, we have automatically generated the implementation for 98 functions (77%). At least one function is implemented for 73 out of 93 constructions (78%).

5 Analysis of the Initial Results

We conducted two evaluations, manual and automatic, to determine whether the automatically implemented functions can successfully parse the respective Swedish constructions and whether they

	Functions	Examples	Exemplified functions
Implemented	51	57	24
Pending	13	16	6
Total	64	73	30

Table 3: Statistics of the manually compiled test corpus: the number of examples belonging to the implemented and pending concrete functions in the generated construction grammar, and the number of functions having at least one test example.

	Functions	Examples	Exemplified functions
Implemented	98	224	65
Pending	29	40	11
Total	127	264	76

Table 4: Statistics of the automatically acquired test corpus. Compare to Table 3.

can cope with different linguistic phenomena. The manual evaluation was based on a subset of selected VP constructions and selected examples from the annotated sentences in SweCcn. The automatic evaluation was based on the whole SweCcn dataset of all VP constructions.

For the manual evaluation, we complied a small test corpus containing 73 annotated examples, of which 57 turned out to have a corresponding concrete function in the construction grammar. Table 3 summarizes the total number of examples that belong to any of the implemented functions and the total number of examples that belong to the functions whose implementation is pending, as well as the number of functions that have at least one test example. In the manually compiled corpus, only about half of the functions have at least one test example, and for those that have, there are two examples on average.

Out of the 57 examples that have a corresponding concrete function, 53 examples were successfully parsed yielding a coverage of 93%. It is important to mention that the relatively high coverage is achieved partially because we replaced all the compounds and proper names which were missing in the lexicon (17 words in total). The remaining 7% are examples for which no parse tree was returned. A closer look at those cases unveils that the parser mostly failed because of: (i) annotation errors in the SweCcn database, for instance, a feature matrix constrains the singular form of a NP although the plural form exists among the annotated examples; (ii) ill-formed sentences (with respect to the grammar), often containing coordinating conjunctions, for instance, *jag och min sambo ska till våra vänner* 'me and my partner shall to our friends' – the parser expects a verb such as *gå* 'go' after *ska* 'shall'.

Errors grounded in the manual annotation of the SweCcn entries were reported to SweCcn developers and are already partially corrected. Errors grounded in the automatic grammar generation require a closer analysis of how these constructions can be systematically implemented using lower level means of RGL.

For the automatic evaluation, we implemented a script which pre-processes the annotated SweCcn sentences belonging to the VP constructions and parses each example using the generated GF grammar. Several heuristics on how to insert the subject to make a proper clause before it is parsed are applied. Heuristics mainly concern the tense and type of the verb given a construction with which it should be parsed. Table 4 summarizes the automatically acquired test corpus.

Out of the 224 examples for which the corresponding concrete function is implemented, 157 were successfully parsed, yielding a coverage of 70%. An investigation of the examples that failed to parse unveils that these examples: (i) contain multi-word compounds; (ii) are more than 10 words long, containing irrelevant phrases and punctuations that fall outside the construction; (iii) contain complex syntactic structures that involve coordination and subordination.

Our analysis shows that many of the failures lead to false negative evaluation results. To avoid these and to allow for a more adequate evaluation, there are several complementary options we have to consider. First, the grammatical categories could be included in the annotated examples, but it depends on the SweCcn developers. Second, we could prepare a treebank, at least one abstract tree for each function, to allow for the opposite testing – to check if the functions generate correct linearizations. Third, we could manually derive a larger post-edited test corpus from the SweCcn dataset of annotated examples. For functions having no test example, we might exploit the GF's built-in support for generating random trees. The linearizations could then be presented to SweCcn developers for examination and consideration of whether an example should be added to the database.

When it comes to the lexicon, the coverage of lexical units is very high. Most of the words the parser fails with are proper names and compounds. These could be extracted from the SweCcn corpus and added to the lexicon if access to the grammatical categories is available.

6 Conclusions and Future Work

We have taken a functional view to acquire a computational construction grammar in Grammatical Framework from the semi-formal representation of the Swedish Constructicon. We have presented an approach to detect and correct inconsistencies and errors in the original resource of constructions. We were able to improve the quality of the resource and thereby increase its value for the use in language technology applications.

Following the proposed approach, the implementation of a construction grammar can be automatically generated for nearly 80% of the constructions (functions) achieving a 70–90% accuracy, and there is clear space for improvement. However, it is still an open question how far we should advance the automation in order to keep it cost effective; the rest can be implemented or post-edited manually. So far we have avoided any manual intervention in the generated grammar because SweCcn is being actively improved and extended in parallel to our work, and this would complicate the synchronisation of changes.

Regarding future work, a rather short-term goal is to extend the grammar generator to cover the other major types of constructions as well. This would primarily require the extension of the auxiliary code generating grammar. Among the long-term goals is to take this approach from the monolingual construction grammar to a multilingual one. This would require not only taking the links to FrameNet into account but also adapting the processing and generation pipeline to the constructicons of other languages. This also relates to our previous research on implementing a multilingual FrameNet-based grammar in GF (Dannélls and Gruzitis, 2014). The GF construction grammar and FrameNet grammar approaches are complementary to each other, at least with regard to constructions with a referential meaning, and an integration of them would be mutually beneficial.

Acknowledgements

This work was supported by Swedish Research Council under Grant No. 2012-5746 (Reliable Multilingual Digital Communication) and by the Centre for Language Technology in Gothenburg.

References

Linnéa Bäckström, Benjamin Lyngfelt, and Emma Sköldberg. 2014. Towards interlingual constructicography. On correspondence between constructicon resources for English and Swedish. *Frames, constructions and computation. Special issue of Constructions and Frames*, 6(1).

Benjamin K. Bergen and Nancy Chang. 2013. Embodied Construction Grammar. In *The Oxford Handbook of Construction Grammar*.

Hans C. Boas and Ivan A. Sag, editors. 2012. *Sign-based Construction Grammar*. CSLI Publications.

Lars Borin, Dana Dannélls, Markus Forsberg, Maria Toporowska Gronostaj, and Dimitrios Kokkinakis. 2010. The past meets the present in Swedish FrameNet++. In *Proceedings of EURALEX*.

Lars Borin, Markus Forsberg, and Lennart Lönngren. 2013. SALDO: a touch of yin to WordNet's yang. *Language Resources and Evaluation*, 47(4).

Dana Dannélls and Normunds Gruzitis. 2014. Extracting a bilingual semantic grammar from FrameNet-annotated corpora. In *Proceedings of LREC*.

Adele E. Goldberg. 2013. Constructionist approaches. In *The Oxford Handbook of Construction Grammar*.

Benjamin Lyngfelt, Lars Borin, Markus Forsberg, Julia Prentice, Rudolf Rydstedt, Emma Sköldberg, and Sofia Tingsell. 2012. Adding a constructicon to the Swedish resource network of Språkbanken. In *Proceedings of KONVENS*.

Carl Pollard and Ivan A. Sag. 1994. *Head-Driven Phrase Structure Grammar*. University of Chicago Press.

Aarne Ranta. 2004. Grammatical Framework, a type-theoretical grammar formalism. *Journal of Functional Programming*, 14(2).

Aarne Ranta. 2009. The GF Resource Grammar Library. *LiLT*, 2(2).

Luc Steels. 2013. Fluid Construction Grammar. In *The Oxford Handbook of Construction Grammar*.

Tiago Timponi Torrent, Ludmila Meireles Lage, Thais Fernandes Sampaio, Tatiane da Silva Tavares, and Ely Edison da Silva Matos. 2014. Revisiting border conflicts between FrameNet and Construction Grammar. *Constructions and Frames*, 6(1).

Representing Honorifics via Individual Constraints

Sanghoun Song
Division of Linguistics and Multilingual Studies
Nanyang Technological University
Singapore
sanghoun@ntu.edu.sg

Abstract

Within the context of grammar engineering, modelling honorifics has been regarded as one of the components for improving machine translation and anaphora resolution. Using the HPSG and MRS framework, this paper provides a computational model of honorifics. The present study incorporates the honorific information into the meaning representation system via Individual Constraints with an eye toward semantics-based processing.

1 Introduction

Honorific forms express the speaker's social attitude to others and also indicate the social ranks of the participants in the discourse and the intimacy. Because honorifics are crucial for using the language in a socially correct way, they have been studied in computational linguistics as well as theories of grammar. Particularly, using the honorific information improves anaphora resolution, and helps machine translation systems provide more natural-seeming output sentences (Mima et al., 1997; Siegel, 2000; Nariyama et al., 2005).

This paper provides a way of modelling honorifics within the formalism of grammar-based language processing. Building upon Head-driven Phrase Structure Grammar (Pollard and Sag, 1994, HPSG) and Minimal Recursion Semantics (Copestake et al., 2005, MRS), the present study suggests using Individual CONStraints (henceforth, ICONS) for representing honorifics from the perspective of multilingual processing.

This paper is structured as follows: Section 2 presents some background knowledge of the current study. Section 3 proposes using Individual Constraints for modelling the honorific system. Building upon the specification, Section 4 shows how honorific expressions can be translated across different honorific types of languages. Section 5 reports a small experiment to see if the current model contributes to semantics-based processing.

2 Background

2.1 Forms of Expressing Honorifics

A cross-linguistic survey reveals that there are three ways of expressing honorifics (Agha, 1994; Ide, 2005): (i) pronouns, (ii) inflection, and (iii) suppletives. Different languages use a different range of honorific systems, but it appears that there exists a hierarchy in the system of honorification, as presented in Table 1. Note that some languages (e.g. English) use no honorific forms.

Table 1: Honorification hierarchy

no forms <	pronouns <	inflection <	suppletives
English, ...			
	Chinese, German, ...		
		Javanese, Hindi, ...	
			Japanese, Korean, ...

The most widespread linguistic phenomenon regarding honorific expressions can be found in the taxonomy of personal pronouns. In many languages, personal pronouns (particularly, second pronouns) are dualized, viz. ordinary (a.k.a. informal) forms and honorific (a.k.a. formal) forms. For example, Chinese employs two second personal pronouns: 你 *nǐ* and 您 *nín*. Both sentences provided in (1) convey a meaning like "What is your name?" in English.

(1) a. 你/您 叫 什么 名字 ?
nǐ/nín jiào shénme míngzi ?
2.SG be.called what name PU

b. #你/您 贵 姓 ?
nǐ/nín guì xìng ?
2.SG noble last.name PU [cmn]

(1a) is a plain way to ask someone's name, in which both pronouns can be felicitously used. In contrast, (1b) is a way of asking in a courteous manner, in which the use of 你 *nǐ* is inappropriate.

Proceedings of the Grammar Engineering Across Frameworks (GEAF) Workshop, 53rd Annual Meeting of the ACL and 7th IJCNLP, pages 57–64,
Beijing, China, July 26-31, 2015. ©2015 Association for Computational Linguistics

That is to say, the predicate in (1b) 贵姓 *guìxìng* is a marked expression in terms of honorification.

Some languages employ a more complicated honorific system. In Japanese, Korean, Javanese, Hindi, and some other languages, the inflectional paradigm is conditioned by the honorific relations between dialogue participants (Siegel, 2000; Ohtake and Yamamoto, 2001; Kim and Sells, 2007). For instance, in Japanese and Korean, if the subject is in the honorific form, the predicate is preferred to be in the honorific form, as exemplified in (2). Note that 先生 *sensei* 'teacher' is an honorific word, and the verbal form *o*+STEM+*ni naru* is used to signify honor to the subject.

(2)

先生	は	本	を	お読み	になり	ました
sensei	wa	hon	o	o-yomi	ni nari	mashi-ta
teacher	TOP	book	ACC	HON-read	become	HON-PST

'The teacher read a book.' [jpn] (Dalrymple, 2001, p. 18)

Other elements can also be marked with respect to honorification. When non-subjects (e.g. objects and obliques) are honored, the canonical verbal form in Japanese is *o*+STEM+*suru*. When the speaker wants to express an honor to the hearer in Japanese, a verbal ending *masu* is used as shown in the last word of (2). On the other hand, the nominal inflectional system is also influenced by honorifics, as exemplified in (3).

(3) a.

お元気	です	か
o-genki	desu	ka
HON-good.health	COP	QUES

'How are you (honored)?'

b.

私	は	元気	です
watashi	wa	genki	desu
1.SG	TOP	good.health	COP

'I am fine.' [jpn]

In (3a), the addressee is presumed to be an honored person, and thereby the prefix *o-* canonically co-occurs with *genki* 'good.health'. In contrast, (3b) explains the speaker's own status, and thereby the honorific marker *o-* does not appear.

Some languages, such as Korean and Japanese, make ample use of suppletive forms of honorification. For example, Japanese has three verbs for 'eat': 食べる *taberu* (neutral), 召し上がる *meshiagaru* '(An honoree) eats', and 頂く *itadaku* '(An honorer) eats'. These suppletive forms can often be used with the inflectional forms mentioned before; for example, お-召し上がり-になる *o-meshiagari-ni naru* '(Someone highly respected) eats' (Nariyama et al., 2005, p. 93-94). Therefore, a single expression can involve all three types of honorification, as shown in (4).

(4)

책을	드리셨습니다.
chayk-ul	tuli-si-ess-supni-ta
book-ACC	give(HON)-HON-PST-HON-DECL

'(An honoree) gave a book (to another honoree).' (The hearer is also an honoree.) [kor]

The verb in (4) contains three honorific forms for the object, the subject, and the addressee. The lexeme 드리- *tuli-* is a suppletive counterpart of 주- *cwu-* 'give'. This verb implies the receiver is respectable. The second one is the suffix *-si-*, which indicates the subject is an honoree. The third one is the ending suffix *-supni-*, which indicates that the speaker expresses a respect to the hearer.

There are also nominal suppletive forms. The different lexical items that denote the same referent sometimes indicate the relative degree of familiarity to the referent. For example, kinship terms in Japanese vary depending on the relationship between the speaker and the referent: When talking about the speaker's own grandfather with others in a modest attitude, 祖父 *sofu* is normally used. When either denoting the other's grandfather or calling the speaker's grandfather friendly and informally, お爺さん *o-jii-san* is normally used. This contrast shows that *o-jii-san* lexically involves an honorific information, whereas *sofu* is neutral. On the other hand, because *o-jii-san* can be used to denote both the other's grandfather and the speaker's own grandfather, the honorific information has to be flexibly represented so as to cover the two potential relations.

In addition to the forms discussed hitherto, some particular constructions, such as passives and interrogatives, can serve to express honorification. However, the meaning is just pragmatically conveyed in this case. Such a construction is not a necessary condition but a sufficient condition for expressing honorifics. Not all passive sentences in Japanese necessarily involve an honorific relation. In contrast, if the *o*+STEM+*ni naru* form in Japanese is used, then the subject is presumed to be an honoree. Since the current work is exclusively concerned with honorific forms, these constructions are out of the scope of this paper.

2.2 Motivations

Honorifics have often been regarded as agreement phenomena just as the subject-predicate agreement in many European languages (Boeckx, 2006;

Kim et al., 2006). However, there is an opposing view to this (Choe, 2004; Bobaljik and Yatsushiro, 2006; Kim and Sells, 2007). One counterexample is provided in (5).

(5) 김선생님이 오(시)었다
Kim-sensayng-nim-i o-(si)-ess-ta
Kim-teacher-HON-NOM come-(HON)-PST-DECL

'Teacher Kim came.' [kor] (Choe, 2004, p. 546)

The subject of (5) contains an honorific form 님 *nim*, but the predicate optionally takes the honorific marker 시 *-si-* though the verb with the honorific marker sounds more natural. Along this line, the current study does not constrain honorification as a way of agreement.

There are also a couple of reasons for not following honorification-as-agreement. These reasons make it necessary to model honorifics as flexibly as possible.

First, honorification is a matter of tendency rather than restriction. Notice that tendency and restriction are not on a par with each other in grammar engineering. Corpus data provide more than a few cases in which a mismatch of honorific forms happens, as exemplified in (5). Grammar engineering systems must work robustly for even less frequent items if the forms appear in naturally occurring texts and unless they critically violate the principle of human language.

Second, honorification is a matter of acceptability rather than grammaticality. Acceptability is primarily concerned with appropriateness, whereas grammaticality confirms the linguistic rules mostly provided by linguists. Thus, acceptability distinguishes not grammatical and ungrammatical sentences, but felicitous and infelicitous ones. In a similar vein, Zaenen et al. (2004) argue that animacy is mainly relevant to acceptability: For instance, the choice between the Saxon genetive and the *of*-genetive in English is sensitive to animacy, but the difference has more to do with felicity. The same goes for honorification. The choice of honorific forms leads to a difference in acceptability which forms a continuous spectrum.

3 Individual Constraints on Honorifics

Minimal Recursion Semantics is the formalism employed to compute semantic compositionality in the present work. In addition, the current work employs ICONS (Individual CONStraints) in order to incorporate discourse-related phenomena into semantic representation of human language sentences. The representation method used in the present study (i.e. MRS+ICONS) has to do with not only semantic information incrementally gathered up to the parse tree, but also other components required to be accessed in the process of cross-lingual processing. MRS+ICONS enables us to model several discourse-related items within an intrasentential system (i.e. sentence-based processing). Notice that there exist several discourse-related items that can be at least partially resolved without seeing adjacent sentences. This can be conceptualized in the format of Dependency MRS (Copestake, 2009), as exemplified in (6).

(6) a. *John likes himself.*
x1 *x2* [*x1* **eq** *x2*]

b. *John likes him.*
x1 *x2* [*x1* **neq** *x2*]

Himself in (6a) equals the subject *John*, while *him* in (6b) does not. The notation in the bracket in each example indicates the relationship between two individuals: **eq**ual and **n**on-**eq**ual. That is to say, anaphora can be partially identified within an intrasentential domain via such a binary relation. There are some other phenomena that require contextual information in theory but can be partially resolved in practice in a way similar to (6), and honorification is one of them.

The current work represents honorifics as a binary relation between two individual elements. A set of honorific information is stored into a bag of constraints, and the value is only partially specified unless there is a clue to identify the honorific relation within the intrasentential context.

3.1 Comparision to Previous Approaches

On the one hand, MRS+ICONS makes honorification (basically a pragmatic information) visible in semantic representation with an eye toward semantics-based language processing. In the previous HPSG-based studies, honorifics are treated as a typed feature structure under CTXT (ConTeXT). This local structure includes C-INDICES whose components are SPEAKER and ADDRESSEE (Siegel, 2000; Kim et al., 2006). In the LFG-based studies, honorification is regarded as an F-structure, given that it is one of the reliable tests to diagnose subjecthood (Dalrymple, 2001). Outside the scope of grammar-based deep processing, several studies make use of shallow processing techniques, such as POS-based pattern matching rules and regular expressions, for paraphrasing honorific expressions (Ohtake and Yamamoto, 2001, among others). In sum, no previous approach represents honorifics into a (near) logical form. In the semantics-based processing, all components that have a part in transfer and generation must be accessed in semantic representation.

On the other hand, the current model provides computational flexibility for handling honorification. Many previous studies on honorification employ a syntactic and/or semantic feature [HON *bool*] (Kim et al., 2006, among others). However, this feature is sometimes misleading for computational processing of honorifics for three reasons. First, there exist more than a few mismatches between honorific forms in real texts written in Korean and Japanese (i.e. no honorification-as-agreement (Choe, 2004)). [HON *bool*] is too restrictive to analyze rather infelicitous but acceptable honorific expressions (§2.2). For example, the two types of second personal pronouns in Chinese are interchangeable in many cases as provided in (1a), and the use of the informal pronoun 你 *nǐ* in (1b) merely results in infelicity (not ungrammaticality). The current work deals with honorifics grounded upon the premise "parsing robustly, generating strictly" (Bond et al., 2008). All potential honorific forms can be parsed robustly and flexibly, but the generation outputs are made strictly and felicitously. Second, [HON *bool*] cannot fully reflect the fact that honorifics are sometimes ambiguous and the specific meaning can be incrementally resolved up to the parse tree (Kim and Sells, 2007). For example, お爺さん *o-jii-san* 'elderly man' in Japanese can be used either informally or formally, and the choice between them depends on syntactic configuration. The current work makes use of a type hierarchy to constrain honorifics (see Figure 1), which manipulates the potential ambiguity and identifies the meaning throughout unification of structures. Third, the Boolean feature is too crude to place different types of constraints on subjects, objects, and addressee. For instance, the verb of (4) (in Korean) includes three HON glosses, and they have different honorific relations. MRS+ICONS represents honorifics as a binary relation amongst individuals, such as speaker, hearer, and referents.

3.2 Fundamentals

MRS+ICONS is structured as shown in (7). The value type is *icons* whose components are IARG1 and IARG2. Since ICONS stands for a binary relation between two individuals, their value type is *individual* (a supertype of *event* and *ref-ind*).

(7)
```
[mrs+icons
  HOOK   [hook
          GTOP          handle
          LTOP          handle
          INDEX         individual
          XARG          individual
          ICONS-KEY     icons
          SPEAKER-KEY   ref-ind
          HEARER-KEY    ref-ind ]
  RELS   diff-list
  HCONS  diff-list
  ICONS  < ! ..., [icons
                   IARG1  individual
                   IARG2  individual], ... ! > ]
```

On the other hand, the HOOK structure, which keeps track of the features that need to be externally visible upon semantic composition, has three additional attributes, viz. ICONS-KEY, SPEAKER-KEY, and HEARER-KEY. These features function like a pointer in the compositional construction of the semantic structure. They are required to mark the constituent analyzed as the speaker or the hearer of an utterance and deliver the information up to the parse tree. In particular, first and second personal pronouns specify this value as their own index (§3.4).

CTXT (under *local*) includes C-INDICES just as Jacy does (Siegel, 2000), but the names are different as presented in the following AVM. Note that the counterpart of "speaker" must be "hearer", and that of "addressee" must be "addressor". The value type is *ref-ind*, because the speaker and the hearer are also referential individuals.

(8)
```
[local
  CAT   cat
  CONT  mrs
  CTXT  [ACTIVATED  bool
         PRESUP     diff-list
         C-INDICES  [SPEAKER  ref-ind
                     HEARER   ref-ind]]]
```

The values of SPEAKER and HEARER remain underspecified until an utterance is established. The typed feature structure of *utterance* is presented in (9), in which SPEAKER-KEY and HEARER-KEY under CONT (i.e. *mrs*) are co-indexed with SPEAKER and HEARER under CTXT. Unless the SPEKER-KEY and the HEARER-KEY are assigned a specific value during the construction of the parse tree, the values are still left underspecified. If the value is not specified until an utterance is built up, that means that the speaker and the hearer cannot be identified within the intrasentential domain.

(9) 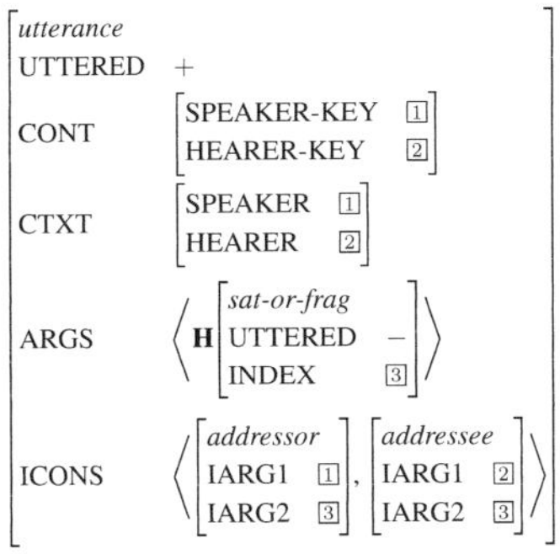

The *utterance* rule syntactically forms a non-branching root node, whose daughter is either a saturated sentence or a fragment (*sat-or-frag*). This pseudo phrase structure rule introduces two elements into the ICONS list, as shown at the bottom of (9). They are valued as *addressor* (i.e. speaker) and *addressee* (i.e. hearer). These ICONS elements play the key role to make dialogue participants visible in semantic representation. Their IARG1s are respectively co-indexed with SPEAKER and HEARER (i.e. [1] and [2]), and the IARG2 are commonly co-indexed with the semantic head's INDEX of the utterance (i.e. [3]). The main reason why they have a relation to the semantic head is that it is necessary to resolve the speaker/hearer scope in quotations. For example, (10) contains two different discourse frames, viz. inner frame and outer frame.

(10) "You have been cruelly used," said Holmes.

The two different frames may have different speakers and different hearers. For instance, the speaker in the inner frame of (10) is Holmes, while that in the outer frame is the narrator of the story. In other words, (10) includes two different utterances, and each introduces its own *addressee* and *addressor* elements into the ICONS list (i.e. four ICONS elements, in total).

3.3 Type Hierarchy

Going into the details, the type hierarchy of *icons* for honorification is sketched out in Figure 1.

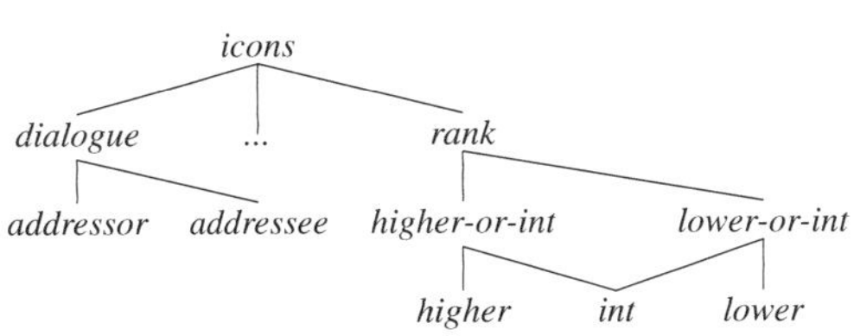

Figure 1: Type hierarchy of *icons*

Regarding honorification, *icons* includes two immediate subtypes: namely, *dialogue* and *rank*. The former branches out into *addressor* and *addressee*, and the latter includes two levels of subtypes. *Higher-or-int* indicates that one individual is socially higher than the other or intimate to the other. Recall that お爺さん *o-jii-san* in Japanese can be canonically used when the referent is higher than the speaker (formal) or intimate to the speaker (less formal). The word itself has the [ICONS-KEY *higher-or-int*] feature, which can be further constrained by the value that the predicate assigns to the word. Honorification is normally relevant to which is "higher" than which, but the linguistic forms can sometimes be altered when talking to someone in the lower position. For instance, Korean employs six levels of imperative inflections conditioned by the relationship between the speaker and the hearer. *Lower-or-int* and *lower* work for this case. Finally, note that *int* inherits from both *higher-or-int* and *lower-or-int*.

3.4 Specifications

First, pronouns are specified with respect to the speaker and the hearer, as shown in (11).

(11) 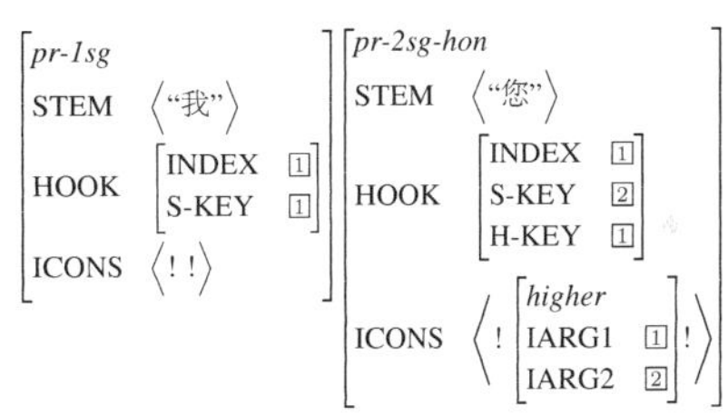

The first personal pronoun has a co-index between its own INDEX and SPEAKER-KEY, and the ICONS list is empty because it does not contribute to honorification by itself. Likewise, the second personal pronouns link their INDEX to HEARER-KEY. If the pronoun is honorific, one ICONS element is introduced. Otherwise (e.g. 你 *nǐ*), the ICONS list is empty. The ICONS element of the right AVM indicates that the hearer [1] is higher than the speaker [2].

Second, several inflectional rules introduce an ICONS element as exemplified in (12) for the subject-honorific form and the addressee-honorific form in Japanese. The left AVM's ICONS element represents that the subject [1] is higher than the speaker [3]. Likewise, the right AVM's ICONS element specifies the relation between the hearer [2] and the speaker [1].

(12) [*ninaru* STEM ⟨"に", "なる"⟩, SUBJ ⟨[INDEX [1], I-KEY [2]]⟩, S-KEY [3], ICONS ⟨! [2] [*higher* IARG1 [1], IARG2 [3]] !⟩] [*masu* STEM ⟨"ます"⟩, S-KEY [1], H-KEY [2], ICONS ⟨! [*higher* IARG1 [2], IARG2 [1]] !⟩]

Third, the suppletive forms themselves do not introduce an ICONS element, but the ICONS-KEY is specified in order to place a partial constrain on polarity. This pointer value functions similarly to [HON *bool*], but operates more flexibly (§3.1). They are instantiated in (13). Note that お休み *oyasumi* is a suppletive counterpart of 寝る *neru* 'sleep' in Japanese.

(13) a. [*sofu* STEM ⟨"祖父"⟩, ICONS ⟨! !⟩] [*neru* STEM ⟨"寝る"⟩, ICONS ⟨! !⟩]

b. [*ojiisan* STEM ⟨"お爺さん"⟩, I-KEY *higher-or-int*, ICONS ⟨! !⟩] [*oyasumi* STEM ⟨"お休み"⟩, I-KEY *higher*, ICONS ⟨! !⟩]

While the neutral forms provided in (13a) are underspecified, the honorific forms in (13b) place a constraint on ICONS-KEY. Notably, お爺さん *o-jii-san* 'elderly man' in Japanese assigns *higher-or-int* to the ICNOS-KEY covering the ambiguity.

3.5 Sample Representation

The example sentence is illustrated in (14). Note that the nominative marker が *ga* and the two verbal ending forms are semantically empty.

(14)

お爺さん	が	お休み	に なり	ます
o-jiisan	ga	o-yasumi	ni nari	masu
HON-elderly.man	NOM	HON-sleep	become	HON

'The elderly man is sleeping.' (to an honoree) [jpn]

Therefore, only underlined elements are left in the semantic representation as shown in (15a). In addition, there are two invisible elements as provided in (15b), such as the speaker and the hearer. Recall that MRS+ICONS includes these invisible referential individuals into the semantics. These four individuals have four relations as presented in (15c), and they are added into the ICONS list.

(15) a. *ojiisan* *oyasumi*
$x1$ $e2$

b. speaker: $x3$, hearer: $x4$

c. [$x3$ ***addressor*** $e2$] (utterance)
[$x4$ ***addressee*** $e2$] (utterance)
[$x4$ ***higher*** $x3$] (ます *masu*)
[$x1$ ***higher*** $x3$] (に なる *ni naru*)

Each relation given in (15c) is in the format as [α **X** β], which is read as "α has an **X** relation to β". For instance, [$x1$ ***higher*** $x3$] means that $x1$ (i.e. the subject) is higher than $x3$ (i.e. the speaker). The first two relations are introduced when the utterance is built up (see (9)). The last two relations came from the verbal ending forms (see (12)). The MRS representation for (14) is provided in (16), in which IARG1 and IARG2 respectively correspond to α and β in the [α **X** β] format.

(16) [INDEX [2],
RELS ⟨[*udef_q_rel* LBL [4], ARG0 [3], RSTR [5], BODY [6]], [*_ojiisan_n_1_rel* LBL [7], ARG0 [3]], [*_oyasumi_s_2_rel* LBL [1], ARG0 [2], ARG1 [3]]⟩,
HCONS ⟨[*qeq* HARG [5], LARG [7]]⟩,
ICONS ⟨[*addressor* IARG1 [8], IARG2 [2]], [*addressee* IARG1 [9], IARG2 [2]], [*higher* IARG1 [9], IARG2 [8]], [*higher* IARG1 [3], IARG2 [8]]⟩]

The traditional representation (16) can be converted into a dependency graph for ease of exposition. In (17), ☺ and ☻ tentatively stand for the dialogue participants.

(17)

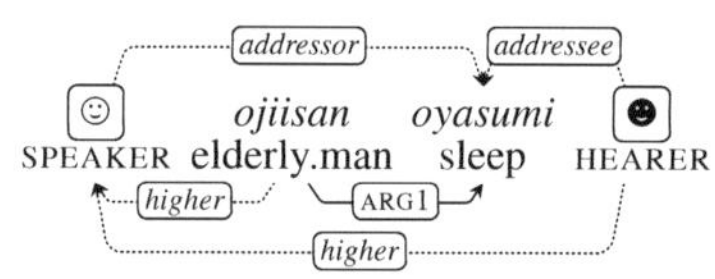

The solid line in (17) means that the relation is specified in the RELS list. The dotted line stands for the ICONS element. The relational value is labelled on the arrow, and the direction of the arrow indicates which individual is co-indexed with which IARG. For instance, the arrow from *ojiisan* to ☺ means the same as [$x1$ ***higher*** $x3$] presented in (15c) and the last ICONS element of (16).

4 Translating Honorifics

With respect to translating honorific expressions across languages, there are different types of translation strategies. Notice that paraphrasing is regarded as a specific type of translation (i.e. monolingual translation) in the current study, given that it is also carried out via the same procedure consisting of parsing, (transfer), and generation.

First, if both the source language and the target language have a complex honorific system (e.g. Japanese→Japanese), all ICONS elements gathered in the parsing stage persist in the transfer and generation stage. The four sentences in Japanese provided in (18) convey a meaning like "Did you/someone sleep?" in English, but the preference in the choice hinges on the social relation. The felicity condition is presented in Table 2.

Table 2: Choice of (18a-d)

	higher subject	plain subject
higher hearer	(18a)	(18b)
plain hearer	(18c)	(18d)

(18) a. お休み になり まし た か ?
o-yasumi ni nari mashi ta ka ?
HON-sleep become HON PST QUES PU

b. 寝 まし た か ?
ne mashi ta ka ?
sleep HON PST QUES PU

c. お休み になっ た ?
o-yasumi ni nat ta ?
HON-sleep become PST PU

d. 寝 た ?
ne ta ?
sleep PST PU [jpn]

The monolingual translation (i.e. paraphrasing) is carried out as follows: First, if a suppletive form is used (e.g. *oyasumi*), the corresponding form in the generation output should be the same because the suppletive form is more informative and specific than the neutral form. If suppletives are converted into neutrals, loss of information happens. Notice that the suppletive forms normally have different PRED names as shown earlier in (15-17). For this reason, (18a-b) and (18c-d) are not interchangeable. Second, if there is an element in the ICONS list of the input MRS, the element persists in the output MRS in order not to lose a piece of information. In other words, a completely underspecified output for each ICONS element is not allowed in generation. For instance, both (18a) and (18c) use *oyasumi* (suppletive), but (18a) cannot be paraphrased into (18c) because (18a) has one more honorific relation in the ICONS list (i.e. *ni naru*). The same goes for (18b) and (18d): Since *masu* in (18b) makes the sentence more informative than (18d), (18b) cannot be paraphrased into (18d). Third, the opposite direction is acceptable. Even if a constituent introduces no ICONS element, the output can include an honorific constituent. For instance, (18c) can be paraphrased into (18a), and (18d) can be paraphrased into (18b). Translating from a less informative form to a more informative form is plausible because there is no discarded information.

Second, if the source language has rich honorifics, and the target language places an honorific constraint on only pronouns (e.g. Japanese→Chinese), the ICONS elements are selectively transferred: The element not linked to pronouns are filtered out. In the opposite direction, the underspecified ICONS element in the input MRS can be resolved in the output as discussed above. For instance, the subject and the hearer in (19) is the honorific second pronoun 您 *nín* in Chinese. (19) cannot be translated into (18c-d) in which *masu* does not show up (see (12)). In contrast, all sentences given in (18) can be translated into (19) without loss of information. Recall that the current model analyzes the neutral form as underspecified (not [HON −]).

(19) 您 睡 了 吗 ?
nín shuì le ma ?
2.SG(HON) sleep PERF QUES PU [cmn]

Third, if the source language employs rich honorification and the target language has no honorific form (e.g. English), the transfer system turns off ICONS. For example, (18a-d) are commonly translated into "Did you sleep?" in English. The other direction (e.g. English→Japanese) raises no problem because all underspecified elements are restored on the target language's side.

5 Experiment

In order to verify whether the current model works for semantics-based processing, one experiment was conducted with ACE (`http://sweaglesw.org/linguistics/ace`). The HPSG used for this experiment is the Jacy (Siegel and Bender, 2002). The basic analysis for honorific expressions in Japanese discussed in this paper was implemented. The testset was the first 4,500 sentences in the Tanaka corpus (Tanaka, 2001). Using these resources, paraphrasing in Japanese (i.e. monolingual translation) was carried out with the 5-best option for parsing and 512MB memory capacity. After paraphrasing was completed, the two results (i.e. without or with ICONS) were compared, as provided in Table 3. The comparison was made with respect to (A) the average output numbers, (B) the number of the items with end-to-end-success, and (C) the number of the items with exact-match-output out of (B).

Table 3: Evaluation

(A, #)		(B, %)		(C, %)	
plain	ICONS	plain	ICONS	plain	ICONS
132.67	280.98	50.38	45.40	59.64	67.89

Table 3 presents that the current model aids in producing more precise outputs, as indicated in (C): The translation accuracy grows by 8.25%. The number of outputs (A) also grows because all potential forms of expressing honorifics are generated without loss of information: All ambiguous interpretations are generated as long as the information is provided in the semantic representation. The end-to-end-success rate (B) decreases, but it is mainly due to the memory limitation, not the model itself: If the size of generated outputs exceeds the given value of memory limitation (512MB in the current experiment), all the outputs are ignored in comparison. If a bigger value is chosen, this rate also increases though it takes much longer time to yield the outputs.

Acknowledgments

I am very grateful to Francis Bond, Jae-Woong Choe, Yasunari Harada, Jong-Bok Kim, Michael Wayne Goodman, David Moeljadi, and Zhenzhen Fan for their help and comments. This research was supported in part by the MOE Tier 2 grant *That's what you meant: a Rich Representation for Manipulation of Meaning* (MOE ARC41/13).

References

Asif Agha. 1994. Honorification. *Annual Review of Anthropology*, pages 277–302.

Jonathan David Bobaljik and Kazuko Yatsushiro. 2006. Problems with Honorification-as-Agreement in Japanese: A Reply to Boeckx & Niinuma. *Natural Language & Linguistic Theory*, 24(2):355–384.

Cedric Boeckx. 2006. Honorification as Agreement. *Natural Language & Linguistic Theory*, 24(2):385–398.

Francis Bond, Eric Nichols, Darren Scott Appling, and Michael Paul. 2008. Improving Statistical Machine Translation by Paraphrasing the Training Data. In *Proceedings of the International Workshop on Spoken Language Translation*, pages 150–157, Hawaii.

Jae-Woong Choe. 2004. Obligatory Honorification and the Honorific Feature. *Studies in Generative Grammar*, 14(4):545–559.

Ann Copestake, Dan Flickinger, Carl Pollard, and Ivan A. Sag. 2005. Minimal Recursion Semantics: An Introduction. *Research on Language & Computation*, 3(4):281–332.

Ann Copestake. 2009. Slacker Semantics: Why Superficiality, Dependency and Avoidance of Commitment can be the Right Way to Go. In *Proceedings of the 12th Conference of the European Chapter of the ACL (EACL 2009)*, pages 1–9, Athens.

Mary Dalrymple. 2001. *Lexical Functional Grammar*. Academic Press, New York.

Sachiko Ide. 2005. How and Why Honorifics can Signify Dignity and Elegance. In Robin Tolmach Lakoff and Sachiko Ide, editors, *Broadening the Horizon of Linguistic Politeness*, pages 45–64. John Benjamins Publishing.

Jong-Bok Kim and Peter Sells. 2007. Korean Honorification: a Kind of Expressive Meaning. *Journal of East Asian Linguistics*, 16(4):303–336.

Jong-Bok Kim, Peter Sells, and Jaehyung Yang. 2006. Parsing Korean Honorification Phenomena in a Typed Feature Structure Grammar. In Luc Lamontagne and Mario Marchand, editors, *Advances in Artificial Intelligence*, pages 254–265. Springer.

Hideki Mima, Osamu Furuse, and Hitoshi Iida. 1997. A Situation-based Approach to Spoken Dialog Translation Between Different Social Roles. In *Seventh International Conference on Theoretical and Methodological Issues in Machine Translation: TMI-97*, pages 176–183, Santa-Fe.

Shigeko Nariyama, Hiromi Nakaiwa, and Melanie Siegel. 2005. Annotating Honorifics Denoting Social Ranking of Referents. In *Proceedings of the 6th International Workshop on Linguistically Interpreted Corpora (LINC-05)*, pages 91–100, Jeju.

Kiyonori Ohtake and Kazuhide Yamamoto. 2001. Paraphrasing Honorifics. In *Workshop Proceedings of Automatic Paraphrasing: Theories and Applications*, pages 13–20, Jeju.

Carl Pollard and Ivan A. Sag. 1994. *Head-Driven Phrase Structure Grammar*. The University of Chicago Press, Chicago, IL.

Melanie Siegel and Emily M. Bender. 2002. Efficient Deep Processing of Japanese. In *Proceedings of the 3rd Workshop on Asian Language Resources and International Standardization*, pages 1–8, Taipei.

Melanie Siegel. 2000. Japanese Honorification in an HPSG Framework. In *Proceedings of the 14th Pacific Asia Conference on Language, Information and Computation*, page 289–300, Tokyo.

Yasuhito Tanaka. 2001. Compilation of a Multilingual Corpus. In *Proceedings of the PACLING*, pages 265–268, Kyushu.

Annie Zaenen, Jean Carletta, Gregory Garretson, Joan Bresnan, Andrew Koontz-Garboden, Tatiana Nikitina, M Catherine O'Connor, and Tom Wasow. 2004. Animacy Encoding in English: why and how. In *Proceedings of the 2004 ACL Workshop on Discourse Annotation*, pages 118–125, Stroudsburg.

Resumption and Extraction in an Implemented HPSG of Hausa

Berthold Crysmann
CNRS, Laboratoire de linguistique formelle (UMR 7110)
Université Paris Diderot (Paris 7),
Case 7031, 5 rue Thomas, F-75205 Paris cedex 13
crysmann@linguist.univ-paris-diderot.fr

Abstract

In this paper, we describe the treatment of extraction in HaG, an emerging computational grammar of Hausa, concentrating on the intricate patterns of interaction between resumptive and gap strategies. We shall argue with Tuller (1986) that Hausa resumption (both overt and covert) opens up the possibility for relativisation only to escape well-attested extraction islands in the language. As suggested by the mutual compatibility of gaps and resumptives in ATB extraction, however, we shall conclude that both strategies must be regarded as unbounded dependencies (UDCs) to be modelled via the SLASH feature in HPSG. We shall discuss how the treatment of UDCs has been generalised, in HaG, to permit more than one simultaneous SLASH dependency, and focus in particular on how the distinction between true gaps and resumptive SLASH elements can be exploited to address efficiency issues.

1 Resumptives and gaps in Hausa extraction

Like many other languages, Hausa makes use of extraction in a variety of constructions, including relative clause formation, matrix and embedded wh-questions, and focus fronting. Alongside gap strategies, familiar from English, Hausa also employs resumption, marking the extraction site with a pronominal.

(1) wā̀ ka àuri 'ya *(-r -sà) ?
who 2.M.CMPL marry daughter.F -of.F-3.S.M
'Whose daughter did you marry?' (Jaggar, 2001)

(2) sàndā sukà dṑkē shì dà *(ita)
stick 3P.CPL beat 3S.DO with 3S.F
'It was a stick they beat him with.' (Jaggar, 2001)

The distribution of gaps and resumptives partly overlap: while in some contexts only a resumptive strategy is possible, e.g. with possessors of nouns (1), or with complements of non-locative prepositions (2), extraction of core arguments (direct/indirect objects) in general permits both strategies, with a clear preference for zero expression in the case of direct objects (Newman, 2000; Jaggar, 2001) for short extraction.

(3) mutā̀nên dà sukà ƙi sayar musù / wà ∅ dà
men REL 3.P.CPL refuse sell to.them / to with
àbinci sukà fìta
food 3.P.CPL left
'the men they refused to sell food to left.' (Jaggar, 2001, p. 534)

As stated by Crysmann (2012), the preference for direct object gaps, however, is much reduced in slightly more complex cases, involving, e.g. Across-The-Board (ATB) extraction or long-distance relativisation (see the discussion below), making resumption a natural, if not the only option. As shown in (4), an overt resumptive is retained in the second conjunct.

(4) [àbōkī-n-ā]$_i$ dà [[na zìyartā̀ ∅$_i$] àmmā
friend-L-1.S.GEN REL 1.S.CPL visit but
[bàn sā̀mē shì$_i$ à gidā ba]]
1.S.NEG.CPL find 3.S.M.DO at home NEG
'my friend that I visited but did not find at home' (Newman, 2000, p. 539)

Example (4) further illustrates that extraction from coordinate structures in Hausa appears to treat resumptives on a par with gaps, as far as the ATB constraint is concerned. Another important observation relates to the possibility of ATB extraction to target different grammatical functions in both conjunct, as illustrated in (5).

(5) mùtumìn$_i$ dà na bā shì$_i$ aro-n
man REL 1.S.CPL give 3.S.M.DO lending-L
bàrgō-nā àmmā duk dà hakà ∅$_i$ yakḕ
blanket-L.1.S.G but in spite of that ∅ 3.S.M.CONT
jîn sanyī
feel-L cold
'the man whom I lent my blanket but who still felt cold' (Newman, 2000, p. 540)

Proceedings of the Grammar Engineering Across Frameworks (GEAF) Workshop, 53rd Annual Meeting of the ACL and 7th IJCNLP, pages 65–72,
Beijing, China, July 26-31, 2015. ©2015 Association for Computational Linguistics

A central property of Hausa resumption is that it permits long distance relativisation out of extraction islands: these include relative clauses, embedded wh-clauses, subject clauses, and complement clauses of non-bridge verbs (see Tuller (1986) for the full set of data). We illustrate here on the basis of embedded relative clauses: as shown below, relativisation of an indirect (6) or human direct object (7) out of relatives is fine, provided there is a resumptive in situ.

(6) Gầ tābōbîn$_j$ dà Àli ya san mùtumìn$_i$
here.is cigarettes REL Ali 3.S.M.CPL know man
dà $\emptyset_i$ zâi yī musù$_j$ / *wà $\emptyset_j$ kwālī
REL 3.S.M.FUT do to.them / to $\emptyset$ box
'Here are the cigarettes that Ali knows the man that will make a box for.' (Tuller, 1986, p. 84; tone added)

(7) Gầ mùtumìn$_j$ dà ka ga yārinyàr$_i$ dà $\emptyset_i$
here.is man REL 2.S.M.CPL see girl REL
ta san shì$_j$ / *sanī $\emptyset_j$
3.S.F.CPL know him / know
'Here's the man that you saw the girl that knows him.' (Tuller, 1986, p. 85; tone added)

The grammar of extraction in Hausa heavily interacts with argument drop: as discussed by Tuller (1986), Hausa allows pro drop not only with subjects, but also with non-human direct objects, which receive a specific, i.e. non-generic interpretation (Jaggar, 2001). Subject properties are identified by agreement marking on the discrete TAM markers.

(8) a. Kā ga littāfì-n Mūsa?
2.S.M.CPL see book-of Musa
'Did you see Musa's book?'

b. Ī, nā gan shì. / Ī, nā ganī
Yes 1.S.CPL see 3.S.M Yes 1.S.CPL see
'Yes, I saw it.' (Tuller, 1986, p. 61; tone added)

(9) a. Kā ga ƙanè-n Mūsa?
2.S.M.CPL see brother-of Musa
'Did you see Musa's brother?'

b. Ī, nā gan shì. / *Ī, nā ganī
Yes 1.S.CPL see 3.S.M Yes 1.S.CPL see
'Yes, I saw him.' (Tuller, 1986, p. 62; tone added)

As discovered by Tuller (1986), the possibility for relativisation to escape what are otherwise extraction islands in the language extends from overt resumptives to zero pronominals. I.e., she observes that non-human direct objects, which can be freely pro-dropped, do permit long relativisation out of islands even without an overt resumptive, whereas direct objects with human reference do so only if realised overtly by a direct object pronominal affix.

(10) mùtumìn$_i$ dà ka san littāfìn$_j$ [dà $\emptyset_i$
man REL 2.S.M.CPL know book REL
ya rubùtā $\emptyset_j$]
3.S.M.CPL write
'the man that you know the book (he) wrote' (Tuller, 1986, p. 81)

(11) littāfìn$_i$ dà ka san mùtumìn$_j$ [dà $\emptyset_j$
book REL 2.S.M.CPL know man REL
ya rubùtā $\emptyset_i$]
3.S.M.CPL write
'the book that you know the man who wrote (it)' (Tuller, 1986, p. 81)

The very same can be shown to hold for wh islands: again, relativisation out of wh clauses is possible for subjects, and for non-human direct objects, even without an overt resumptive.

(12) mùtumìn$_i$ dà ka san [mḕ$_j$ $\emptyset_i$ ya
man REL 2.S.M.CPL know what 3.S.M.CPL
rubùtā $\emptyset_j$]
write
'the man that you know what (he) wrote' (Tuller, 1986, p. 80)

(13) littāfìn$_i$ dà ka san [wầ$_j$ $\emptyset_j$ ya rubùtā
book REL 2.S.M.CPL know who 3.S.M.CPL write
$\emptyset_i$]
'the book that you know who wrote (it)' (Tuller, 1986, p. 80)

The converse, however, is not true: wh phrases never extract out of either relative or embedded wh clauses, regardless of the presence of overt or covert resumptives. Examples (14) and (15) illustrates this for subjects and non-human direct objects, whereas (17) provides evidence that resumption (here with an oblique) does not improve acceptability.

(14) * wànè mùtûm$_i$ ka bā nì littāfìn$_j$ dà $\emptyset_i$
which man 2.S.M.CPL give me book REL
ya rubùtā $\emptyset_j$
3.S.M.CPL write
'Which man did you give me the book that wrote' (Tuller, 1986, p. 81; tone added)

(15) * wànè littāfī$_j$ ka san wầ$_i$ $\emptyset_i$ ya
which book 2.S.M.CPL know who 3.S.M.CPL
rubùtā $\emptyset_j$
write
'which book do you know who wrote' (Tuller, 1986, p. 80; tone added)

(16) wầ$_j$ ka yi màganầ dà shī$_j$
who 2.S.M.CPL do talking with 3.S.M
'Who did you talk with?' (Tuller, 1986, p. 158)

(17) * wầ$_j$ ka san mằtâr$_i$ [dà $\emptyset_i$ ta yi
who 2.S.M.CPL know woman REL 3.S.F.CPL do
màganầ dà shī$_j$]
talking with 3.S.M
'Who do you know the woman that talked to him' (Tuller, 1986, p. 159)

The most complex case of long-distance relativisation cited in the literature involves triply embedded relatives, with all three extraction sites contained within the inner-most sub-clause.

(18) ? gằ mằtâr$_i$ dà ka bā nì littāfìn$_j$ dà
here.is woman REL 2S.M.CPL give me book REL
mằlàmai sukà san mùtumìn$_k$ dà $\emptyset_i$ ta
teachers 3P.CPL know man REL 3S.F.CPL
rubū̀tā wà $\emptyset_k$ $\emptyset_j$
write for

'Here's the woman that you gave me the book the teachers know the man she wrote it for.' (Tuller, 1986, p. 84; tone added)

To summarise the empirical data, relativisation in Hausa is insensitive to extraction islands, provided the presence of a resumptive pronoun at the extraction site. Other types of extraction, like wh or focus fronting, do not exhibit this property, regardless of the presence of resumptives. As suggested by extraction from coordinate structures, however, resumptives are fully compatible with gaps, as far as the ATB constraint is concerned. We therefore conclude that both processes should be considered unbounded dependency constructions (UDCs), yet the specific constraints on locality and on the use of gaps vs. resumptives should be associated with properties of the elements at the top or the bottom of the dependency: i.e. the difference between a single relative marker merely mediating coreference with the antecedent noun vs. a full displaced constituent, as well as the nature of the governing head at the extraction site, i.e. verbs vs. prepositions.

1.1 Previous approaches

The first extensive formal study of Hausa extraction and resumption certainly is Tuller's (1986) doctoral dissertation on the language. Using a GB framework she suggests to account for the difference between island-insensitive resumptive relativisation and wh extraction by means of a distinction between base-generation and binding of a pronominal for relativisation vs. Ā movement for wh-extraction. Resumptives found in wh extraction as complements of obliques or possessors of nouns, by contrast, are treated as instances of phonetic trace (Koopman, 1984). The multitude of analytic devices (both base generation and movement with phonetic trace) for what appears to be a single phenomenon (resumption) has been criticised in Crysmann (2012).

Within HPSG, one of the first studies are the works of Nathan Vaillette on resumption in Hebrew (2001a) and Irish (2001b), proposing two separate features for gap and resumptive extractions. This separation has been criticised repeatedly in the HPSG literature, including Taghvaipour (2004; Taghvaipour (2005b; Taghvaipour (2005a), (Alotaibi and Borsley, 2013), and (Crysmann, 2012), mainly based on the known compatibility of gaps and resumptives in ATB extraction.

More specifically, Crysmann (2012) argues, on the basis of the Hausa data, for the compatibility between the two types of extractions. He shows further that no HPSG treatment available at the time was capable to capture the differences with respect to extraction islands. He suggests that both types of unbounded dependencies should be regarded as SLASH dependencies, distinguishing gap and resumptive dependencies in terms of the properties of the SLASH elements. More precisely, he argues that gaps require sharing of entire LOCAL values, whereas sharing of INDEX values is sufficient for resumptives (see Borsley (2010; Alotaibi and Borsley (2013) for a similar proposal). Since the description of resumptives subsumes that of gaps, the ATB facts are readily explained. The differences in locality, however, are due to constraints imposed at the retrieval site: while wh and focus fronting require full sharing of their LOCAL values, relatives merely require index sharing. If retrieval sites are transparent to indices, but not to full local values, the empirical pattern can be explained with a single mechanism.

A previous implementation of resumption in HaG has treated these elements essentially like gaps, including the restriction of SLASH to contain at most one element at any time. In this paper, we shall explore how the empirically and theoretically more desirable approach advanced in Crysmann (2012) can be put to use in a computational grammar of the language.

2 Implementation in LKB & friends

The implementation in HaG follows quite closely the theoretical proposal made in Crysmann (2012). Thus, both gap and resumptive dependencies are represented on SLASH, HPSG's feature for extraction, distinguishing them for the purposes of island effects in terms of the elements rather than by virtue of a distinct unbounded dependency.

2.1 The Grammar Matrix

The LinGO Grammar Matrix (Bender et al., 2002) is a starter kit for the development of HPSG grammars running on the LKB (Copestake, 2002), Pet (Callmeier, 2000) and Ace (by Woodley Packard (Crysmann and Packard, 2012)) platforms. Grammars running on these platforms use a conjunctive subset of TDL (Krieger, 1996) as their description language and Minimal Recursion Semantics (Copestake et al., 2005) for meaning representation. The Grammar Matrix not only makes for fast bootstrapping of new grammars, it also ensures a high degree of parallelism, owing to a carefully worked out constraint set on meaning construction combined with a type hierarchy of rule types, suitable for a wider range of syntactic constructions.

The Matrix has been distilled to a great extent from the LinGO ERG (Copestake and Flickinger, 2000). As for extraction, both the ERG and the Matrix are highly faithful to the theory of unbounded dependencies advanced by Sag (1997) and Ginzburg and Sag (2001): thus, passing of non-local features (most notably SLASH) proceeds in a head-driven fashion, with heads amalgamating the NON-LOCAL values of their arguments.

(19) SLASH amalgamation

$$\begin{bmatrix} \text{SYNSEM} \left[\text{NLOC} \left[\text{SL } \boxed{1} \cup \ldots \cup \boxed{n}\right]\right] \\ \text{ARG-ST} \left\langle \left[\text{NLOC} \left[\text{SL } \boxed{1}\right]\right], \ldots \left[\text{NLOC} \left[\text{SL } \boxed{n}\right]\right] \right\rangle \end{bmatrix}$$

In the ERG and the Matrix, amalgamation is broken down into four constraints depending on the arity of the argument structure list, one of which any lexical head will inherit from. Owing to the absence of sets (and set union) in the underlying formalism, set-valued features are represented by means of difference lists (Clocksin and Mellish, 1981) instead,[1] instead, as shown in the example for two-element argument structure lists in (20).

(20)

$$\begin{bmatrix} \textit{0-diff-list} \\ \text{LIST } \boxed{1} \\ \text{LAST } \boxed{1} \end{bmatrix} \quad \begin{bmatrix} \textit{1-diff-list} \\ \text{LIST } \begin{bmatrix} \text{FIRST } [\,] \\ \text{REST } \boxed{1} \end{bmatrix} \\ \text{LAST } \boxed{1} \end{bmatrix}$$

$$\begin{bmatrix} \textit{basic-two-arg} \\ \text{SYNSEM } \left[\text{NLOC} \left[\text{SL} \begin{bmatrix} \text{LIST } \boxed{1} \\ \text{LAST } \boxed{3} \end{bmatrix}\right]\right] \\ \text{ARG-ST } \left\langle \begin{bmatrix} \text{LIST } \boxed{1} \\ \text{LAST } \boxed{2} \end{bmatrix}, \begin{bmatrix} \text{LIST } \boxed{2} \\ \text{LAST } \boxed{3} \end{bmatrix} \right\rangle \end{bmatrix}$$

Among the lexical amalgamation types, there is already one definition in the Matrix specifically aimed at resumptive pronouns, i.e. the possibility to launch a non-local dependency that does not correspond to an argument. However, this constraint will only ever be suitable for free pronouns, not bound ones, as we find in Hausa, since the type constraint is defined on the level of the lexical entry. Furthermore, resumption is still treated as entirely identical to gap-type extraction.

Besides these more technical issues, there is, however, a more fundamental difference between the treatment of SLASH dependencies in the theoretical HPSG literature and its implementation in the ERG and the Matrix: while Pollard and Sag (1994) clearly argue that more than one element can be in SLASH at the same time, the ERG and the Matrix both limit the length of the SLASH list to at most one, thereby ruling out the combination of strong and weak UDCs witnessed in (21). The reason behind this restriction is most certainly related to processing efficiency.

(21) [A violin this well crafted]$_1$ even [the most difficult sonata]$_2$ will be easy to play $\_{2}$ on $\_e_1$? (Pollard and Sag, 1994, 169)

While for English, cases of multiple simultaneous SLASH dependencies can possibly be marginalised without jeopardising overall coverage on natural language data, this is certainly not the case in a variety of other languages, including multiple wh-fronting in Slavic, or long-distance relativisation in Hausa. Thus, a more systematic solution is called for that we shall develop in the following section.

2.2 Multiple SLASH dependencies

Since HaG is based on the Grammar Matrix, the current general approach to extraction is already head-driven, in accordance with the current consensus amongst HPSG scholars. Since restrictions on the size of SLASH are imposed on introduction and retrieval, we can concentrate on these two critical points in our discussion of extraction in HaG.

2.2.1 Launching

With the exception of adjunct extraction,[2] gaps in HaG are introduced by means of unary *lexical* rules suppressing a valency corresponding to an argument introduced into SLASH, essentially following Pollard and Sag (1994), Sag (1997), Ginzburg and Sag (2001), as well as common practice in the ERG and the Matrix. In addition, a unary *phrase structure* rule permits launching of adjunct extractions.

As for resumptives, the current implementation maintains two sets of lexical rules, one for bound pronominals and one for bound resumptives, as well as two sets of lexical entries for pronominals and resumptives. Making systematic use of the type hierarchy of rules and lexical types, shared properties of resumptive and non-resumptive uses, including autosegmental morphophonological properties, are abstracted out into common supertypes. Most crucially, in the true pronominal case, a semantic relation is inserted into the MRS RELS list and the SLASH

[1] Difference lists permit list concatenation by means of unification: essentially, such lists maintain a pointer (LAST) to the open end of the list. We shall use exclamation marks to distinguish these from ordinary lists, as is the convention in DELPH-IN grammars (Copestake, 2002, cf.).

[2] See Levine (2003) for arguments to distinguish adjunct and complement extraction in English along the syntax/lexicon divide.

value is restricted to be empty, whereas in the resumptive case, the RELS list is empty, but SLASH contains an element the referential index of which is shared with that of the resumptive. Owing to the absence of internal disjunction from the underlying feature formalism (rules and lexical entries are in disjunctive normal form), specification of separate rules and entries for both uses turned out to be unavoidable.[3] In order to keep the number of disjunctive specifications to an absolute minimum, we have therefore generalised the existing 3 sets of morphological rules for pronominal affixation (objective, genitive, dative), capturing the difference in shape by reference to the segmental make-up of the base, rather than in terms of the syntactic category of the base, enabling us to collapse all three sets into one. This move was greatly facilitated by the fact that nouns and verbs, as well as the applicative marker *wà* independently undergo characteristic inflection for the type of argument realisation of their first complement (Crysmann, 2005), distinguishing inter alia realisation by a pronominal affix: e.g., pronominal affixes from the genitive set are always preceded by the gender differentiated linker *-n/-r* (cf. example (1)), a segment that is crucially absent in final positions of all verbs taking pronominal affixes from the direct object set. To account for differences in tonal specification (genitive set is low, whereas objective set alternates), we generalised our previous treatment of "polar" tone with objective pronouns, representing the tonal specification of the pronominal affix as a floating tone of the base. In fact,

Following Crysmann (2012), the main difference between gap and resumptive SLASH values is that the former require reentrancy with a full local value, whereas the latter are underspecified in this respect: minimally, they only require identity of INDEX. Elaborating on the hierarchy of *synsem* proposed in Sag (1997), we have complemented the *gap* subtype of *synsem* with a type for resumptives and abstracted out shared minimal requirements into a common super type.

(22)
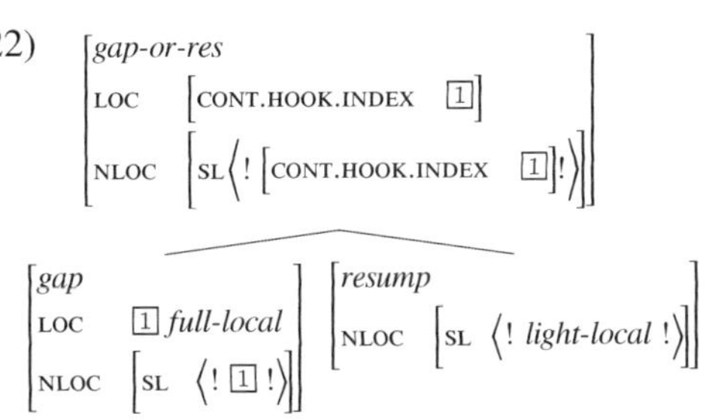

[3] Underspecification techniques using list types do not provide a solution either, since we need to use difference lists for which this abstraction is only available to a limited extent.

(23)
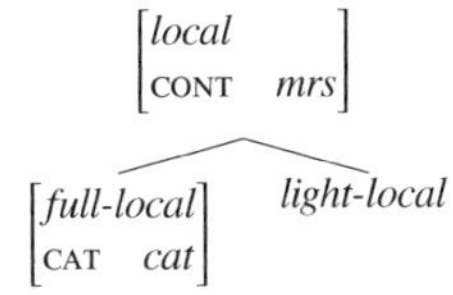

Using the types just introduced, extraction and resumption rules are the defined as follows:

(24) Complement extraction

$$\begin{bmatrix} \text{SS} \left[\text{LOC} \left[\text{CAT} \left[\text{VAL} \left[\text{COMPS} \;\; \boxed{l}\right]\right]\right]\right] \\ \text{DTR} \left[\text{SS} \left[\text{LOC} \left[\text{CAT} \left[\text{VAL} \left[\text{COMPS} \;\; \langle \textit{gap} \mid \boxed{l} \rangle\right]\right]\right]\right]\right] \end{bmatrix}$$

(25) Resumption

$$\begin{bmatrix} \text{SS} \left[\text{LOC} \left[\text{CAT} \left[\text{VAL} \left[\text{COMPS} \;\; \boxed{l}\right]\right]\right]\right] \\ \text{DTR} \left[\text{SS} \left[\text{LOC} \left[\text{CAT} \left[\text{VAL} \left[\text{COMPS} \;\; \langle \textit{gap-or-res} \mid \boxed{l} \rangle\right]\right]\right]\right]\right] \end{bmatrix}$$

Both rules perform a valence reduction, but do so imposing constraints of different strength on the locally suppressed complement. Since elements of the COMPS valence list are reentrant with ARG-ST, the restriction towards SLASH will be picked up correctly by SLASH amalgamation. For resumption, the grammar distinguishes variants for null realisation (subject and non-human direct object) and pronominal affixation.

On the basis of the distinction between *full-local* and *light-local* values, we have furthermore defined typed list constraints that permit to restrict what kind of dependencies can be active simultaneously. As we have seen above, only relativisation can escape wh-islands in Hausa, provided the dependency involves a resumptive. Furthermore, relative clause formation, in contrast to wh-extraction and focus fronting, does not permit pied-piping. Thus, multiple simultaneous SLASH dependencies can involve at most one single gap type dependency at any node. Most importantly, this state of affairs enables us to ensure termination in the light of adjunct extraction which involves true gaps: whenever a true gap is inserted into SLASH, the remainder of the SLASH list is constrained to consist entirely of elements of type *light-local*. Complement extraction lexical rules are constrained in a similar fashion.

2.2.2 Retrieval

Given that SLASH values may contain multiple elements, retrieval at the top of the dependency marks a more clear departure from common practice in the Grammar Matrix: in essence, we need to search the SLASH list for a suitable element to be bound off, and pass on any *light-local* elements to be retrieved further up the tree.

The grammar has exactly two constructions where retrieval can take place, the first one being a classical filler-head construction to be used for binding wh and focus-fronted fillers, both of which allow pied-piping. As for relatives, we follow Borsley and assume that Hausa relative "pronouns" are actually (inflected) relative complementisers that take the clause containing a gap or resumptive as its complement. This assumption not only takes care of the impossibility of pied-piping in relative clauses, but it also captures nicely the similarity of the uninflected relative complementiser *dà* to its homonymous non-relative counterpart. What is common to both constructions is that they define a non-empty TO-BIND value (cf. Pollard and Sag (1994)).[4] In filler-head structures, the SLASH dependency to be retrieved is constrained to be of type *full-local* by virtue of structure sharing with the filler's LOCAL value, whereas no such constraint is imposed by the relative complementiser which only requires a referential index.

(26)
$$\begin{bmatrix} \textit{filler-head-rule} & \\ \text{SS.NLOC} & \begin{bmatrix} \text{T-B} & \begin{bmatrix} \text{FILL} & \langle \boxed{l} \rangle \\ \text{SL} & \boxed{s} \end{bmatrix} \\ \text{SL} & \langle ! \; ! \rangle \end{bmatrix} \\ \text{FILLER-DTR} & \begin{bmatrix} \text{SS} \begin{bmatrix} \text{LOC} & \boxed{l} \end{bmatrix} \end{bmatrix} \\ \text{HD-DTR} & \begin{bmatrix} \text{SS} \begin{bmatrix} \text{NLOC} \begin{bmatrix} \text{SL} & \boxed{s} \end{bmatrix} \end{bmatrix} \end{bmatrix} \end{bmatrix}$$

(27)
$$\begin{bmatrix} \textit{rel-complementiser-lex} & \\ \text{SS} & \begin{bmatrix} \text{NLOC} \begin{bmatrix} \text{T-B} & \begin{bmatrix} \text{FILL} & \left\langle \begin{bmatrix} \text{CONT} \begin{bmatrix} \text{HOOK} \begin{bmatrix} \text{INDEX} & \boxed{i} \end{bmatrix} \end{bmatrix} \end{bmatrix} \right\rangle \\ \text{SL} & \boxed{s} \\ \text{REL} & \langle ! \; \boxed{i} \; \textit{ref-index} \; ! \rangle \end{bmatrix} \\ \text{SL} & \langle ! \; ! \rangle \end{bmatrix} \end{bmatrix} \\ \text{ARG-ST} & \left\langle \text{S} \begin{bmatrix} \text{NLOC} \begin{bmatrix} \text{SL} & \boxed{s} \end{bmatrix} \end{bmatrix} \right\rangle \end{bmatrix}$$

Two unary retrieval rules then take care of binding the filler to an appropriate percolated SLASH element and to pass on any elements of type *light-local*.

(28)
$$\begin{bmatrix} \textit{bind-filler-rule} & \\ \text{SS} & \begin{bmatrix} \text{LOC} & \boxed{0} \\ \text{NLOC} & \begin{bmatrix} \text{T-B} & \begin{bmatrix} \text{FILL} & \langle \rangle \\ \text{SL} & \langle ! \; \boxed{l} \; ! \rangle \end{bmatrix} \\ \text{SL} & \boxed{s} \\ \text{QUE} & \boxed{q} \\ \text{REL} & \boxed{r} \end{bmatrix} \end{bmatrix} \\ \text{ARGS} & \left\langle \text{SS} \begin{bmatrix} \text{LOC} & \boxed{0} \\ \text{NLOC} & \begin{bmatrix} \text{T-B} & \begin{bmatrix} \text{FILL} & \langle \boxed{f} \rangle \\ \text{SL} & \langle ! \; \boxed{f} \mid \boxed{l} \; ! \rangle \end{bmatrix} \\ \text{SL} & \boxed{s} \\ \text{QUE} & \boxed{q} \\ \text{REL} & \boxed{r} \end{bmatrix} \end{bmatrix} \right\rangle \end{bmatrix}$$

(29)
$$\begin{bmatrix} \textit{find-filler-rule} & \\ \text{SS} & \begin{bmatrix} \text{LOC} & \boxed{0} \\ \text{NLOC} & \begin{bmatrix} \text{T-B} & \begin{bmatrix} \text{FILL} & \boxed{f} \\ \text{SL} & \boxed{l} \end{bmatrix} \\ \text{SL} & \langle ! \; \boxed{1} \; \textit{light-local} \mid \boxed{s} \; ! \rangle \\ \text{QUE} & \boxed{q} \\ \text{REL} & \boxed{r} \end{bmatrix} \end{bmatrix} \\ \text{ARGS} & \left\langle \text{SS} \begin{bmatrix} \text{LOC} & \boxed{0} \\ \text{NLOC} & \begin{bmatrix} \text{T-B} & \begin{bmatrix} \text{FILL} & \boxed{f} \\ \text{SL} & \langle ! \; \boxed{1} \mid \boxed{l} \; ! \rangle \end{bmatrix} \\ \text{SL} & \boxed{s} \\ \text{QUE} & \boxed{q} \\ \text{REL} & \boxed{r} \end{bmatrix} \end{bmatrix} \right\rangle \end{bmatrix}$$

While the *bind-filler-rule* performs the actual instantiation and retrieval of the unbounded dependency, the *find-filler-rule* merely iterates over the original SLASH difference list and puts back one by one the original elements, constrained to *light-local*. In essence, these rules jointly ensure the island restriction towards non-resumptive SLASH dependencies: since extraction out of relative and wh islands is restricted to relativisation footed by a resumptive, the constraints on *light-local* for further percolation after the first retrieval of a SLASH element accounts for the ungrammaticality of, e.g. (14) and (15), while still permitting relativisation out of relatives, as witnessed in (18).[5]

[4] All lexical entries other than the relative complementiser require their entire TO-BIND value to be empty (i.e. both TO-BIND.FILL and TO-BIND.SLASH). Furthermore, we constrain the type *head-nexus-phrase* (Sag, 1997) as well as standard unary phrase structure rules to effect structure sharing of TO-BIND between the mother and the (head) daughter. Similarly, elements on ARG-ST are equally restricted to have empty TO-BIND features. As a net effect, no other syntactic rule can interfere in the middle of retrieval.

[5] One might wonder why we insist on full perusal of SL(ASH), even after a filler has been found, instead of merely constraining the remainder of the list using the aforementioned list types. First, this recursion does not add any complexity factor beyond the possibility of that introduced by considering alternative instantiations for the filler. Second, recreating the SLASH list recursively step by step from the unretrieved elements enables us to get rid of any latent constraints on the open end of the list regarding *local* type: once we have retrieved a *full-local* dependency, we want to be able to add new gap dependencies further

2.2.3 ATB extraction

The underspecification approach to resumptives, i.e. their compatibility with both *light-local* and *full-local*, already ensures the compatibility between true gaps and resumption in ATB extraction from coordinated structures. Furthermore, given the ambiguity of pronominals between resumptive and true pronoun uses, identity requirements will only have to hold for those pronominals that actually enter in a non-local dependency.

To this end, we restrict coordinating constructions to enforce identity of entire SLASH lists, as shown in (30).

(30)
$$\begin{bmatrix} \textit{s-binary-coord} & \\ \text{SYNSEM} \begin{bmatrix}\text{NLOC} \begin{bmatrix}\text{SL} & \boxed{S}\end{bmatrix}\end{bmatrix} & \\ \text{LCONJ-DTR} & \begin{bmatrix}\text{SYNSEM} \begin{bmatrix}\text{NLOC} \begin{bmatrix}\text{SL} & \boxed{S}\end{bmatrix}\end{bmatrix}\end{bmatrix} \\ \text{RCONJ-DTR} & \begin{bmatrix}\text{SYNSEM} \begin{bmatrix}\text{NLOC} \begin{bmatrix}\text{SL} & \boxed{S}\end{bmatrix}\end{bmatrix}\end{bmatrix} \end{bmatrix}$$

A complicating factor, however, comes in owing to the use of lists, instead of sets, imposed by the underlying formalism. As detailed in Newman (2000), ATB extraction may target different grammatical functions in both conjuncts. Since Hausa also permits multiple relativisation from the same clause (Tuller, 1986), we expect multiple ATB relativisation to be possible also with reversal of grammatical functions, as illustrated by the (constructed) example in (31).

(31) gà mùtûm dà kukà san mā̀târ
there.is man.M REL you.PL.CPL know woman.DEF.F
dà yakḕ sôn -tà àmmā takḕ
REL 3.S.M.CONT like.VN.of -3.S.F but 3.S.F.CONT
ƙîn -sà
hate.VN.of -3.S.M
'Here's the man that you know the woman who he likes but (who) hates him.'

In order to allow for this possibility, we complement the standard coordination schema sketched above with an alternative one that has the first elements of the right conjunct reversed.

For efficiency reasons, I am currently limiting myself to permutation of the first two SLASH elements. This decision, however, is supported by the observation that triple relativisation in itself is already considered marked to some extent: see Tuller's question mark on the relevant example in (18). While these data clearly contrast with the unacceptability of island violations, I seriously doubt that their marked acceptability will improve when combined with ATB extraction from non-parallel conjuncts, thereby further increasing complexity. Thus, until we have evidence to the contrary, I shall refrain, for the time being, from full permutation of SLASH lists greater than 2, assuming parallelism of dependencies except for the first two elements.

up the tree, independently of whether this new SLASH element will be prepended or appended to our current SLASH list.

3 Conclusion

We have argued in this paper that Hausa extraction militates for an extension of current practice in HPSG grammar implementation to permit multiple simultaneous SLASH dependencies. Based on the theoretical proposal by Crysmann (2012), we have provided an implementation of the Hausa extraction facts. In essence, we have generalised the constraints on SLASH to permit multiple members at any time, but have systematically exploited the distinction between light and full local values to constrain multiple extraction to involve at most on gap simultaneously. This not only correctly captures the island constraints in Hausa, but it also provides a straightforward means to ensure efficiency, including termination of adjunct extraction. Furthermore, to keep disjunctive specifications of pronominal and resumptive uses to a minimum, we have developed a more generalised treatment of pronominal affixation in the language, collapsing morphological rules for genitive accusative and dative pronominal affixes. In future work, we shall explore how the systematic ambiguity between resumptive and non-resumptive uses of pronominals may be captured without disjunctive specification at all, in order to provide a complete answer to McCloskey's (2002) generalisation.

Acknowledgements

Work on HaG is partially supported by the French National Research Agency (ANR) as part of the "Investissements d'Avenir" programme (reference: ANR-10-LABX-0083), project ResHau [re:'zo:] of the Laboratoire d'excéllence "Empirical Foundations of Linguistics".

References

Mansour Alotaibi and Robert D. Borsley. 2013. Gaps and resumptive pronouns in Modern Standard Arabic. In Stefan Müller, editor, *Proceedings of the 20th International Conference on Head-Driven Phrase Structure Grammar, Freie Universität Berlin*, pages 6–26.

Emily M. Bender, Dan Flickinger, and Stephan Oepen. 2002. The grammar matrix: An open-source starter-kit for the rapid development of cross-linguistically consistent broad-coverage precision grammar. In John Carroll, Nelleke Oostdijk, and Richard Sutcliffe, editors, *Proceedings of the Workshop on Grammar Engineering and Evaluation at the 19th International Conference on Computational Linguistics*, pages 8–14.

Robert D Borsley. 2010. An HPSG approach to Welsh unbounded dependencies. In Stefan Müller, editor, *Proceedings of the 17th International Conference on Head-Driven Phrase Structure Grammar, Université Paris Diderot, Paris 7, France*, pages 80–100, Stanford, CA. CSLI Publications.

Ulrich Callmeier. 2000. PET — a platform for experimentation with efficient HPSG processing techniques. *Journal of Natural Language Engineering*, 6(1):99–108.

William F. Clocksin and Christopher S. Mellish. 1981. *Programming in Prolog*. Springer, Heidelberg.

Ann Copestake and Dan Flickinger. 2000. An open-source grammar development environment and broad-coverage English grammar using HPSG. In *Proceedings of the Second conference on Language Resources and Evaluation (LREC-2000)*, Athens.

Ann Copestake, Dan Flickinger, Carl Pollard, and Ivan Sag. 2005. Minimal recursion semantics: an introduction. *Research on Language and Computation*, 3(4):281–332.

Ann Copestake. 2002. *Implementing Typed Feature Structure Grammars*. CSLI Publications, Stanford.

Berthold Crysmann and Woodley Packard. 2012. Towards efficient HPSG generation for German, a non-configurational language. In *Proceedings of the 24th International Conference on Computational Linguistics (COLING 2012)*, pages 695–710, Mumbai, India.

Berthold Crysmann. 2005. An inflectional approach to Hausa final vowel shortening. In Geert Booij and Jaap van Marle, editors, *Yearbook of Morphology 2004*, pages 73–112. Kluwer.

Berthold Crysmann. 2012. Resumption and island-hood in Hausa. In Philippe de Groote and Mark-Jan Nederhof, editors, *Formal Grammar. 15th and 16th International Conference on Formal Grammar, FG 2010 Copenhagen, Denmark, August 2010, FG 2011 Ljubljana, Slovenia, August 2011*, volume 7395 of *Lecture Notes in Computer Science*, pages 50–65. Springer.

Jonathan Ginzburg and Ivan Sag. 2001. *Interrogative Investigations: the Form, Meaning and Use of English Interrogatives*. CSLI publications, Stanford.

Philip Jaggar. 2001. *Hausa*. John Benjamins, Amsterdam.

Hilda Koopman. 1984. *The Syntax of Verbs. From Verb Movement Rules in the Kru Languages to Universal Grammar*. Foris, Dordrecht.

Hans-Ulrich Krieger. 1996. *TDL — A Type Description Language for Constraint-Based Grammars*, volume 2 of *Saarbrücken Dissertations in Computational Linguistics and Language Technology*. DFKI GmbH, Saarbrücken.

Robert D. Levine. 2003. Adjunct valents: cumulative scoping adverbial constructions and impossible descriptions. In Jongbok Kim and Stephen Wechsler, editors, *The Proceedings of the 9th International Conference on Head-Driven Phrase Structure Grammar*, pages 209–232, Stanford. CSLI Publications.

James McCloskey. 2002. Resumptives, successive cyclicity, and the locality of operations. In Samuel David Epstein and T. Daniel Seely, editors, *Derivation and Explanation in the Minimalist Program*, pages 184–226. Blackwell, Oxford.

Paul Newman. 2000. *The Hausa Language. An Encyclopedic Reference Grammar*. Yale University Press, New Haven, CT.

Carl Pollard and Ivan Sag. 1994. *Head–Driven Phrase Structure Grammar*. CSLI and University of Chicago Press, Stanford.

Ivan Sag. 1997. English relative clause constructions. *Journal of Linguistics*, 33(2):431–484.

Mehran Taghvaipour. 2004. An HPSG analysis of Persian relative clauses. In Stefan Müller, editor, *Proceedings of the HPSG-2004 Conference, Center for Computational Linguistics, Katholieke Universiteit Leuven*, pages 274–293. CSLI Publications, Stanford.

Mehran Taghvaipour. 2005a. *Persian Relative Clauses in Head-driven Phrase Structure Grammar*. Ph.D. thesis, University of Essex.

Mehran A Taghvaipour. 2005b. Persian free relatives. In Stefan Müller, editor, *The Proceedings of the 12th International Conference on Head-Driven Phrase Structure Grammar, Department of Informatics, University of Lisbon*, pages 364–374, Stanford. CSLI Publications.

Laurice A. Tuller. 1986. *Bijective Relations in Universal Grammar and the Syntax of Hausa*. Ph.D. thesis, UCLA, Ann Arbor.

Nathan Vaillette. 2001a. Hebrew relative clauses in HPSG. In Dan Flickinger and Andreas Kathol, editors, *The Proceedings of the 7th International Conference on Head-Driven Phrase Structure Grammar*, pages 305–324, Stanford. CSLI Publications.

Nathan Vaillette. 2001b. Irish gaps and resumptive pronouns in HPSG. In Frank Van Eynde, Dorothee Beermann, and Lars Hellan, editors, *The Proceedings of the 8th International Conference on Head-Driven Phrase Structure Grammar*, pages 284–299, Stanford. CSLI Publications.

Author Index